HOOK OF HOPE

HOOK OF HOPE

NURJAHAN KHATUN

NEW DEGREE PRESS

COPYRIGHT © 2021 NURJAHAN KHATUN

HOOK OF HOPE

ISBN   978-1-63730-420-4   *Paperback*
       978-1-63730-497-6   *Kindle Ebook*
       978-1-63730-498-3   *Ebook*

*I would like to dedicate this book to my Baba for gifting
me with his time, however short that may have been. He
is in my every intention, in every heartbeat, and he is the
driving force behind any good that I do in this world.
To my two sisters, who gave me a reason to live when
my younger self was trying to navigate this world.
To all those who were placed at every critical juncture
of my life; you all know who you are as you formed
the loving family that the universe chose for me.
Finally, this book is also dedicated to everyone who has gone
through challenges in their life and felt there was no way out.
To everyone who is currently going through a dark period in
their life and feels like they can't breathe; this will pass.*

CONTENTS

———

AUTHOR'S NOTE   11

CHILDHOOD   15
DEAF AND DUMB   27
BABA   39
HOMELESS   61
LOVE OF LEARNING   71
MARRIAGE   85
DIVORCE   107
CAREER AND SOCIAL IMPACT   127
HOPE   139

ACKNOWLEDGEMENTS   149

"Where there is ruin, there is hope for a treasure."

—RUMI

AUTHOR'S NOTE

My Baba (dad) named me "Nurjahan," which means "bringing light into the world." After he had four boys, I finally came along, and Baba always told me that was why he named me that; I was the light that came into his world. Our elders would say that the name you are given is the person you become. I truly believe in that too. I became, I am, and I continue to be a Nur (light) in everyone's life—helping others, being able to contribute to someone's growth and development, empowering those around me, and giving them hope.

My Baba was always helping others from all walks of life despite not having much himself. He was my rock amongst all the chaos that was around me as I was growing up. Reflecting on my life, it's very clear that everything I strived to achieve was only to make my Baba feel proud of me. Knowing my Baba has my back, spiritually speaking, gives me strength, makes me work hard, work clean, and work with excellence.

A lot of people make assumptions about me because of what I have achieved. Because I come across as strong and independent, people assume I have a supportive network and family. That could not be further from the truth. Growing up in one of the poorest boroughs in London, I was one of the lucky ones to get out of the neighbourhood and make a life for myself. My friends and I grew up in the same poverty-stricken neighbourhood, and we were all from a low socio-economic background. I grabbed opportunities when I saw them, and although those around me had the same opportunities available to them, they did not take up on those opportunities.

I have been fortunate to be afforded opportunities as a public speaker to talk about difficult topics from which my community typically shies away. Whether it is through my role as a volunteer TV presenter, where we talk about domestic abuse or homelessness, or through being a keynote speaker, where I share my personal journey of how—despite the odds—I overcame difficult challenges in my career; I want to educate others and raise awareness of these topics to help drive the right conversations.

By speaking on different platforms, I can connect with people from all walks of life. I always had a flurry of people coming to me to express how much they needed to hear what I had to say and just how pleased they were to see someone to whom they could relate who was brave enough to speak about difficult topics. Often, audiences would suggest I share my story more widely. Each time I spoke and had an impact with the audience, I realised just how important it is to raise awareness around these subjects. There are not enough people from backgrounds like mine who are willing to talk about topics about women and their roles in society in an open, honest, and transparent way and who do not fear the repercussions of hurting egos or making others uncomfortable. For example, I've had encounters where people reject the idea that homelessness exists within the Muslim community.

People remain my number one priority: my passion for the betterment of people around me, whether in my community or at my workplace, shines through my words and actions. That is why having a positive impact on even one person's life is truly something that I hold dear to my heart.

In 2020, I've had nine people reach out to me to tell me that if they had not seen my vlogs, then they would have committed suicide.

To know I can have an impact on even one person and give others hope that they can hold on to is truly humbling. That realisation has driven me to want to make hope accessible to more people. I wanted to let others know what it feels like to have hope and believe in themselves. I have achieved making hope accessible and helping #bringbackhumanity one person at a time. I am able to give others the "hook of hope" so they too believe they can live their dreams. I use this term in my social impact work, whereby providing a safe space for women to dream and realise those dreams, by providing women that hook of hope. By listening to and believing in them, I continue to be their hook of hope. In reality, that is all anyone wants: for someone to believe in them.

I'm a great believer in hope and how we need to anchor ourselves onto hope, not people. Hope has been the golden thread throughout my journey. Hope has enabled me to overcome all of life's challenges.

This book is for anybody going through any kind of struggle and looking for hope. It is for anyone who's looking for a way to become more understanding of somebody else's circumstance, to build empathy and emotional intelligence.

Read this book to remember the importance of talking about topics that make you uncomfortable. If a topic makes us feel uncomfortable, and we're able to hold that conversation for more than a few minutes, then we know we're doing something right.

This book will remind you that we never really know what people are going through unless we ask them—unless we take the time out to listen. My story is inclusive, and you will be able to relate to it. You may even use it to find hope within yourself. I hope I can encourage you to build bridges between communities. Together we will #bringbackhumanity.

CHILDHOOD

———

I grew up in a typical rundown neighbourhood in East London that housed many other Bangladeshi immigrant families. The small block of flats we lived in had six homes on each floor, so there was the ground floor, the first, second, and third floors. The flat I grew up in was one of twenty-four in total in a neighbourhood that was rough—riddled with crime, drugs, and gangs. Four identical blocks like mine with even more social housing were all around us. My family was in flat number twelve, and we were in the corner flat on the first floor.

When my parents first came to this block of flats, they were one of the first set of Bangladeshi families. Over time, more Bangladeshi families moved in. Growing up as a child one of seven siblings where I was fifth in order, I thought it was pretty cool to be on a corner flat as we had views of three sides of the building. It also meant we had a bit more space outside our front door to play games with balls, skipping, chase each other around and spend time in the summer months.

The space outside our front door was a nice spot for a few people to hang out and talk, as I sometimes would with the other young girls who lived in the housing block. My mum used a blue box in the space to grow some vegetables—mostly tomatoes, runner beans, and coriander. The view from that spot looked out to the building in front of us, which was used by the local council. It had a lot of green space—a playing area, football area, and basketball court. Further back, you could see more social housing. We had a great vantage point to witness anything that was happening in the area.

You could not fit more than two people in our kitchen; however, I probably spent most of my time there—not out of choice, mind you. I had multiple roles to fulfil that required me to be in that kitchen at all times. I would have to switch from being the eldest daughter to my parents, to being an older sister to my two kid sisters, to a younger sister to my older brothers, and then (the role I loved most) my Baba's (dad) girl.

That kitchen was in bad condition, overworked, and constantly in use. We could never afford to buy new items. Everything we owned, from clothes and utensils to furniture, was always secondhand. We bought most of our things from the Sunday market, and my visits to the market were my only chance to go out.

I absolutely loved the Sunday market, as it provided the very few times when my mind could wander off, think of anything other than chores, work, and responsibilities, and do something that I was never allowed to do at home: dream.

At Baba's usual light walking speed, the route from home to the bus stop would take around eight minutes. Baba worked six days a week, and he was hardly ever home, so Sundays were the only days any of us got a chance to see him enjoy time off. But Sundays were never really days off because he had to do other chores, like shopping, for our home. It was, however, one of the few times I got to spend time with Baba that was uninterrupted.

He would motion his right hand in a way that indicated I should hold his hand for safety. I would run up, grab his hands, and skip along to the bus stop. I was my happiest then during those years when I was between seven and eleven years of age, my smile beaming from one ear to the other. I would always have my little trainers on with my traditional hand sewn (by my mum) South Asian clothes known as 'shalwar kameez'. That was my bubble. I almost felt as though I was in control of that time and bubble. I did not have to share it with anyone else, other than my brothers, who would also take that trip to the market. As we entered the Sunday market, the smell of freshly fried burgers wafting through the air would catch mine and my brother's attention. It was at that moment we would all say together, "Ahhh, doesn't that smell amazing?" it was a market that sold everything and anything you could think of. The market was very well-known as it had furniture, utensils, clothes, food, and even an entire section where cars would line up and sell items from the boot of their cars. My brothers would often tag along, helping to carry the bags. This was Baba's way of introducing chores and the man's role in the family to them. That market was like a maze, and while Baba bought furniture or cleaning supplies, I would observe the art of haggling.

Baba was great at haggling; he would speak to the men and women at the stalls until he got himself a bargain. I learnt from a young age that you do not always need shiny, brand-new items. As soon as we returned from the market, my Baba would get all of us to sit with a bowl of hot water and soap, and we would clean the items he had purchased until we could see our own reflections. To me, seeing that was like magic. Because recycling and upcycling were so common in my home, those practices have stuck with me. As a result, I learnt to respect items I owned, living within our means and being grateful for what I had.

In my earliest memories of our kitchen, I was six or seven years old and peeling garlic, potatoes, and onions. Baba taught me to cook—unpacking weekly groceries, cutting up fish and meat, and feeding all our neighbours from the biggest pot my arms could handle. A few years later, that one, small kitchen saw me regularly cook for over a hundred people.

The kitchen had a window. Even when I was seven or eight, I would look out through the window and dream of how I would escape the space I was in and beyond the building and treetops. I would wonder what was beyond the places my eyes could see.

Growing up in a very poor inner-city London borough, survival was key to keep our heads above water. My Baba earned little, so money was always tight at home. Most of what we bought was usually secondhand from the Sunday market, also known as the Petticoat Lane market. We had a few new items, but we only purchased them during our Eid, our religious celebration times, which we had two of every year. The first is a celebration after a month of fasting called Ramadan, and the Eid coincides with the holy pilgrimage to Mecca in the Kingdom of Saudi Arabia (KSA). During these occasions, we would go out and buy new clothes to celebrate in. I grew up seeing both parents working, who had responsibilities both here in London and abroad to feed families back home in Bangladesh.

A recent urban study found my borough has the highest rate of poverty, child poverty, unemployment, and pay inequality of any London borough, and it has *always* had these dire statistics. I guess it's common for certain areas to appeal to immigrant communities. My borough attracts large numbers of rural people looking for employment, evidenced by successive waves of foreign immigration. First came Huguenot refugees (French protestants), followed by the Irish, later Ashkenazi Jews, and—in the twentieth century—Bangladeshis. Although no ethnic group forms a majority of the population, Asians form forty-one percent, of which thirty-two percent are Bangladeshi—the largest ethnic minority group in the borough. Like my Baba, many of these immigrants worked in the clothing industry.

The flat we lived in was infested with a zillion cockroaches, and it's incredible that I was not afraid of them. As I got older, I developed a fear of insects, and I would have a heart attack if I saw such level of insect infestation now.

Our three-bedroom flat was always congested and over-crowded with six siblings, both my parents and, at times, one to three guests staying with us for short periods. We all lived in a three-bedroom flat. One of my earliest memories is that I was always the one who ended up sleeping on the floor, instead of in a bed, because of overcrowding. I never quite understood why that was the case. Why was it always me on the floor? Even today, I struggle to sleep on a mattress that is not as hard as a floor.

Both mum and Baba worked hard to give us what they did. Mum was a tailor for over twenty years. She worked on the machine constantly—working twenty-hour days. That meant I was raising my two younger sisters. When my sisters were young, they would play, sleep, and rest on a huge pile of coat linings. We often saw piles of linings dotted around the room where mum would sew and in other bedrooms. We would help pack those into huge bags for transferral, as that was the very last step in the process.

As I mentioned before, one of my earliest memories from as young as six or seven years old was the constant cooking preparation I was responsible for; from the age of eleven, I was the one who was actually doing the cooking for the family. Now, that might sound really strange to anybody reading this, but in Bangladeshi culture, that is very much the norm. From a young age, girls help their mothers with domestic tasks; the eldest daughters typically help around in the kitchen. This was no different for me being brought up in London. When I reflect on this period in my life, I can understand how that was not something most would associate with a young girl growing up in an inner-city London borough. I say this because, now that I have nineteen nieces and nephews, times have changed so much for the better where children are not required nor expected to work as hard as I used to when I was growing up.

There was a positive side to this, though, as all of my siblings had to learn to gain maximum usage of our items, knowing that we did not have the luxury of receiving replacements in a timely fashion. For example, during my high school years, I only had three pairs of underwear to rotate wearing at any one time. They had a white background with pink, yellow, and green horizontal stripes, and the colours were bright. As they were all similar in design, I used to worry about being picked on in primary school if some of the other kids noticed I was wearing the same underwear whilst changing for the physical education sessions.

Growing up in a strict conservative household meant many topics were never spoken about, including anything to do with puberty. So, when I first got my period, it terrified me. I did not know how to tell my mum I was bleeding. A few days in, I was so distraught that I just blurted out to mum that I was bleeding, and she gave me this little rag, said a few words about how to use it, and then got some sanitary pads for me. I always wondered why we could never talk about such important life matters openly in our family. I never quite understood why parents would have kids and never be honest about aspects of life; how to behave, fundamentals of life like puberty, and how to balance Bangladeshi and Muslim cultures. It would explain why so many members of my generation grew up without communication skills—having emotional issues, mental health problems, and the inability to develop, nurture, and grow relationships.

I have had to endure some experiences that were truly traumatic as a direct result of not having healthy relationships and not being able to speak about topics that were viewed as taboo in our Bangladeshi-Muslim community. One of these topics is how your body goes through numerous changes. For example, when I was in high school, I noticed I was experiencing a lot of discomfort and pain around my private area. I could not understand what was happening as I regularly bathed, cleaned myself, and wore clean underwear.

I found I could remedy the problem by using Vicks VapoRub. It sounds crazy that I could not talk to my mother about what I was having to go through or ask to see a doctor, but I would actually use Vicks on my private area. I did this hoping it was going to solve what I now know to be thrush! All South Asians use this rub as we all seem to believe that Vicks can cure everything but death. We always had a tub of Vicks in our home, so it was the only "medicine" I was aware of and could think to use.

Everything just felt so damn difficult growing up in those days because I had no one to go to with questions and nobody would teach me anything—not about how your body goes through so many changes, how a girl steps into womanhood through puberty, or what sex education is. Our culture does not support having open discussions about life lessons like this.

Unlike my classmates, the way I recall the five years I attended secondary school was not by my school timetable but by the schedule of responsibilities I had at home. I attended a mixed-sex school, a Church of England school which was only ten minutes down the road from home. Baba chose it as it was closer, plus he was keen that I learn how to interact with the opposite sex and learn life skills. Mum, however, was not keen on this as she believed I should have attended an all-girls school, but that was slightly further away. Many more Bangladeshi girls also attended the school, but I was only one of a few headscarf-wearing students.

- 7:30 a.m.–wake-up and leave to get to school.
- 9:45 a.m. to 3:15 p.m.–in class.
- 3:30 p.m. to 4:00 p.m.–time to wash, change, and eat.
- From 4:00 p.m. to 7:00 p.m., I had to work on a sewing machine. One of those big, factory-sized machines. I learned how to sew from a very young age, when I started off by learning how to sew in straight lines. My first job was to sew the arm of the lining, and that only required one straight line. That's how my tailoring career kicked off at a tender age of eleven. I absolutely hated it, but I had no choice. I sewed from the age of eleven to sixteen.
- At 7:30 p.m., I needed to get dinner ready. Around 8:30 p.m., Baba would get home from work, and everything

had to be ready and be placed on the mat on the floor, which was a traditional way of eating.

- By 11:00 p.m., everybody had been fed, and I had cleaned everything. Every night was the same routine; I had to clean the entire kitchen, getting on my knees to mop the kitchen floor with little kitchen towels.

By the end of this I would think, *Okay, I've got my homework to do still and the only two places left in the house to sit to get any light to do my homework would be the bathroom or the kitchen.* Each time I would use the light in either of those rooms I'd be told off, my mother saying, "You're wasting electricity," because we could not afford it. We had to be very careful, thinking economically to save on utility bills. Being from a low socio-economic background meant that was life—this was our standard of living, and it was further stretched because anything mum earned went back home to support extended family in Bangladesh. Meanwhile, everything we had in London came from dad's paycheck.

It was quite difficult because that routine I just described went on for pretty much my entire high school life. I was the only sibling out of the six of us who had to sew, cook, clean, and do everything else for our family. I grew up resenting my mum and thinking it was unfair and unjust that my three older brothers and two younger sisters did nothing. I never really had a childhood; I never got to enjoy playing outside or to make friends outside of our home. I used to cry so much, dreading the weekend, where I was forced to sew all-day long! As I got older, Baba told my brothers to do more, and they did bits here and there, but they left most of the chores for me to complete.

I would be forced to be at home "machining away," and I never quite understood why I was always treated differently from my siblings. I was never allowed to do normal "kid" stuff. I was so confused, and it felt like I was being punished. My environment was strict, conservative, and ignorant at times. I can only guess that eldest daughter syndrome in a man's world meant I was expected to do everything. This gender imbalance used to upset me so much. I had to serve my brothers. They got to eat first, wash first, talk first, *everything* first. They were able to do a chore for a few minutes and run away. I could never do that. I would be rushed back and get a telling off or a beating.

I grew up hating the fact that I was born a girl. When I was younger—even from a very early age—I wanted to look like my brothers, just so I could be treated as an equal, as one of them. I could get some attention, some love, just something. Hell, I would have been happy with some crumbs thrown my way. I wanted to dress the same as my brothers, tried wearing their clothes, and I wanted my hair to be just as short as theirs so I could fit in and be one of them. I never got the attention I wanted. I never got the love I craved like my brothers did. Despite doing my best to look like my brothers, I never did fit in. I did the opposite, I think; I confused my family because I was fighting so hard to be like my brothers when, in fact, I was a girl. That meant my life trajectory had to be different from that of my brothers. The reason I grew up a tomboy and the reason I wanted to learn to box from my brothers was to try to fit in and be closer to them.

I always thought to myself, *There's got to be more to life than this*. I grew up seeing women in our community on a strict trajectory - getting married, having children, and being stuck in cooking and cleaning like slaves. I never saw the women in my home, neighbourhood, or community be anything else. I just could not understand why that was. That has stuck with me my entire life. That shaped me, drove me, and gave me the fire in my belly to do more, do better, be more, be better.

I wanted to feel that I could learn from my own experiences; I wanted to have the decision of how I dress, what I think, who I interact with, what I eat, when I eat, how I eat—whether it is with my hands, a spoon, or a fork. Oh, to be able to make those simple, basic decisions that every other person around me takes for granted.

When we had dinner, I was not allowed to eat fresh food as I was responsible for making sure that everyone else was fed first whilst mum was working. I was also taught not to waste food, so when everyone finished eating, I would have to eat everyone's leftovers before I could eat any fresh food. Traditionally, we eat with our bare hands, and if I dared to eat with a spoon or fork, then I would be labelled as a "coconut" and asked why I was trying to be "special" or "different."

I was never allowed to express myself through what I wore; I had to be modest. My mum dictated how I dressed. She stitched all our (South Asian) clothes. I only started to wear "normal" (Western) clothes once I went to the Church of England high school. If what I chose to wear was too short, I would get told off and a slap across the face by either my mum or my brothers. If I wanted to express myself and wear some makeup that my neighbour introduced me to, my brothers would play police and beat me for doing so. There would be times during festival times where neighbouring girls would apply lipstick on me and I would really enjoy wearing it. As soon as my brothers saw that, then they would physically hit me and force me to remove it from my face. Incidents like those made me feel sad, worthless, and less of a girl.

They reserved the harsh treatment for only me, as none of my siblings had to go through this.

My younger sisters had a good relationship with my mother and the rest of the family, as they were young and could do nothing wrong. As the elder sister, I was responsible for making sure my behaviour modelled "perfection" so they would not be led astray. I had never been envious of my sisters because I helped to bring them up and was almost a motherly figure to them. My relationship with them both has always been strong and still is to this day.

My mother did not let me interact with anyone, even the young girls who lived in the same block of flats as us. My interaction with them was very limited. I can only guess that she did not want me to be influenced by them in any way, or maybe she wanted to reduce the possibility that I would share my home experiences with anyone outside the family. This was part of the reason I grew up believing my mother was not my biological mother.

DEAF AND DUMB

When I was younger, from the age of six upwards, I was always laughing loudly and smiling. I was loud and boisterous, which was out of character according to my community. As a young Muslim girl, I was expected to always remain quiet and dutiful. It was therefore expected that I would not be seen laughing and joking around. I was also very tall for my age, which meant I always I looked older than I was. Yet another thing for others to talk about (like I was not in front of them), for them to pick, dissect, and pass judgement on.

As I laughed and joked around quite often and was therefore seen as disobedient. When I did laugh and joke around, I was taking a risk of being disciplined, which usually meant either being told off or physically suffering the consequence of my actions. I was always told I would never amount to anything in my life. There's a Bengali word that was used by my family initially and then by the wider community to describe me: "Owah." The best way to translate it into English is a combination of being deaf and dumb.

"Owah" is a very derogatory term. My family had aspirations for my siblings to become doctors, lawyers, etc. But I was told that I would become nothing. I was going to be yet another Bangladeshi woman who would bear children and spend long days and nights toiling in a kitchen. Because of my friendly, loud character coupled with the very strict and conservative environment in which I was raised, I was immediately condemned to never achieving anything in my life. As that was the leading opinion of me in my immediate family, my extended family would know me for that too. This opinion later extended to the wider community.

It was so strange how everyone was constantly judging me, concluding what I would become or not become, even before I was a teenager. It made me feel like I was stuck in a soundproof glass room. No matter how hard or how loud I screamed to say, "I am more. I can be more. I am not deaf and dumb. I have feelings. Do not talk about me in that way," no one could hear me. I made the movement with my mouth and went through the motion of screaming, but there was no sound. No one heard me, and no one even noticed I was waving my arms, begging to be heard, begging to be accepted for me, and begging everyone to stop labelling me.

If I was invisible at home, 'a nobody' at my high school amongst my friends, I was loved. It seemed like almost everyone wanted to be my friend and to spend time with me. I excelled academically and was very well-liked by students and teachers alike. I became known as the girl who looked after everyone and was the "head girl" each year. School became my safe space where I could slowly begin to express myself. I now had a little more control in terms of who I befriended and how I interacted with others. It felt like new territory, as I had not had enough experience in this setting.

Everybody at home and those from my community were incredibly dismissive of me, and that was difficult for me to come to terms with, especially since I had done nothing to deserve that type of treatment. The impact that their words and actions had on me was quite substantial; when you're told something over and over again, soon enough you start to believe them.

In my case, I started to believe that I was nothing, that I was "owah," that I would never be my own person. For example, when I could not cook dishes to my mother's standards, I would be told how I was good for nothing. She would ask why I could not remember that I should have put a particular ingredient in or why I did not cook it on low heat for longer. Those moments hurt and saddened me immensely as each time I cooked I would pray so hard to get it one hundred percent right, just in the hope that my mother would finally say it was good. I just wanted a little assurance from her that I, at eleven or twelve years old, was meeting her standards. I guess it was a way of wanting to feel loved and cared for—to feel I was worthy in her eyes.

I was constantly trying to impress and make my mother happy. There were times when I would run to the kitchen before being told to, thinking that would make my mum happy as I was showing initiative and being proactive. I would cook, thinking I had cooked something amazing without making any mistakes, but then I would be reminded that I did in fact make a mistake. Those moments made me cry so much. I felt like I had failed. I failed to secure some love for which I was so desperately longing.

Because I was always told that I was a failure and that I could never get anything right, I ended up believing that I would never amount to anything—that my destiny was to get married as soon as possible, to bear children, and to cook and clean. I was to serve everybody except myself, doing whatever I needed to do to make everybody around me happy—except myself.

That is the notion I grew up with. That is what I was effectively told by everyone, and I learned this through people's mannerism, interactions, and behaviour towards me. Everyone told me I was a big fat zero. I would never be anything useful, never be of use to myself. I was told that if I was not bearing children, that if I was not cooking, if I was not running a kitchen, then there would be no hope for me. They said I had no other purpose; if I am not doing any of those, then why exist?

My parents, my siblings, my neighbours, and the broader community constantly berated me and girls like me, and every time I heard this, it felt like I was being punched in the stomach. Word got out very early on that I was going to be nothing, that I was deaf and dumb, that I was "owah." Word got out that I had no potential, that I would never be successful in anything. Word got out because I stutter, because it takes a little longer for me than my siblings to get a certain point across, that there was not a hope in hell for me.

The nickname "Owah" was catching on. I was no longer Nurjahan. I was now "Owah."

Outside of school, my identity was non-existent. I was never Nurjahan Khatun, who was a great girl, who had a happy personality, and who was excelling in school. No. Rather, I was reduced to a mistake for being born a girl. Then, I was never good enough in general—not a good enough young Muslim girl. I could never do anything right, and I was made to know that at every opportunity. Nobody called me by my pet name, Nuri. Nobody called me Nurjahan. I was reduced from a child, a young girl, to a thing, or even what felt like nothing. I was now just plain "Owah." I was no longer a person; I was stripped of anything and everything that identified me as Nurjahan.

At that time, I could not comprehend how important identity was going to be to me. I never understood how, without an identity, I would always remain nothing.

Later, as I entered adulthood, I started to learn, question, and absorb why having a sense of identity is important. Adulthood allowed me to stand out as an individual, to develop a sense of being and importance, and to fit in with certain groups and cultures. As humans, we express a sense of identity through verbal and nonverbal means, including language, clothing, and social status. Identity has a strong biological origin and plays an important role too. Identity exists in many forms. It ranges from small traits to powerful behaviours. Speech, ideas, sound, hair style, and type of clothing are examples that can communicate identity to help people develop attachments to like-minded individuals.

Certain thoughts and beliefs, such as religious values, are broad-reaching ideas surrounding a sense of identity. Identity is such a vast subject, and it is integral to who one is, yet I felt I was deprived of all that. Identity was confining for me—limiting, hurtful, full of judgement, not about possibility, self-actualization, etc. I was given a very clear and unforgiving definition of my identity—and felt to fail at every moment. I was not embraced for the amazing individual that I am. I was not allowed to flourish and to learn.

I always saw that identity was an opportunity. The concept of identity for me is something that encapsulates one's experiences, something that is not constant, something that is uncertain and impermanent, and something that continually shifts. For me, a person can have multiple identities according to the opinions and values of those who may wish to identify as an "individual" or a supposed "self." Your identity evolves as you evolve as a person, as you grow and develop. Growth and development are a natural consequence of life because I am changing as a person as I live each day and my ideas change and my opinions form and re-form.

Identity is the very essence of my existence. Every culture has things associated with it: name, reputation, traits, habits, abilities, minds, and appearances. In my view, all of these things together give a person a sense of purpose, yet I was denied all of that. I feel like I was robbed. I feel like I have not fully grown, although my physical appearance says I have.

My own lack of identity meant I could never think beyond what I was told to think and feel. What could I ever become? What could I ever achieve? And by that very definition, I could not dream, I could never think beyond where I lived, I could never see beyond my community and the bubble I was in. My eyes looked through that kitchen window, but at those times, I felt I would never see beyond that. I experienced so much anxiety as a young girl that I was going to be part of another statistic, be another woman who would bear children and run a kitchen. My life was laid out for me.

As a young child, my stutter reinforced to everyone that I was "Owah." I always had difficulty pushing my words out. I truly believe that part of the reason I stuttered was because I was in constant fear. It may be because of the fear that I would not do things right, fear of being told off, fear of failing at something because no matter how well I did something, I would still be told that I did not do it correctly. That instilled the fear of life in me; my hands would shake, my whole body would shake, and my voice would shake before I attempted to do any task.

The moments when this stutter was magnified were those times when I would hear my name being called and I was summoned to a room either where my mother was or, worse, where neighbours gathered. For example, when there was an audience, when I was getting told off for not cleaning properly, or when I was expected to respond to a question, my stammering would immediately kick in. I would start to sweat, feel anxious, and hope that I would not be beaten because of some mistake I had made.

One Sunday afternoon, many of the ladies gathered at our flat to have lunch together, and I did something as simple as forgetting to heat up a curry and bring it out. I was screamed at in front of everyone. I wanted to curl up and have the ground swallow me up because of the embarrassment of being screamed at. When I was expected to respond, I was unable to as my stuttering would kick in full force; I could feel the words floating in my mind and mouth, but I could not push the words out—only some weird sounds. I felt I could not breathe, and my heart was going to explode out of my chest. It would take me a while to recover from moments like that.

I really believe that my stuttering stemmed from fear (though there is no science behind my assessment of the situation). It will be really hard for people to believe, but I used to stutter all the time, until I went to university.

I would typically start to stutter when my siblings would blame me for things that were naughty in order to avoid getting in trouble with my mother. Each time, before getting a slap or a telling off from my mother, I was unable to explain the truth, as the words never came out of my mouth. In my attempts to speak, noise would come out instead. My stuttering was another reason I was called deaf and dumb; I couldn't speak in a coherent manner.

I lived in a constant state of anxiety from the age of six until my Baba passed away when I was sixteen. I was never allowed to be myself, as I was always on edge. This was especially true when my Arabic/Quran teacher would give feedback about my recitation of the holy book. My words were heavy on my tongue, and I struggled to recite properly. None of my other siblings had this issue, and I was the only child who needed extra support, feeding into the narrative that I was stupid. This provided many the opportunity to say negative things about me and to me.

Weekday evenings after school we would attend classes to learn Arabic and I used to be beaten by the Quran teacher when I was not able to recite my reading fully and completely by the end of the session. Sadly, this was very much the accepted norm back in those days. I was hit badly because I couldn't push the words out, could not articulate the words that I was reading in Arabic. As my recitation would slow down, my stuttering got in the way, resulting in a delay to my Arabic learning. My stuttering proved to everyone around me that I must be different. It was so hard for me to express myself, so hard to say what I wanted to say, because I could never push out a word. It all got stuck, and instead, I would make this sort of motoring noise where a bunch of nothingness was coming out of my mouth. Just noise, like a car engine failing to start day in, day out. So, the abuse of being told that I was worthless continued during those Quran classes.

Day in, day out—being told, "Nurjahan, you're dumb."
Day in, day out—being told I'm stupid.
Day in, day out—being told I have no cognitive ability.
Day in, day out—being told I would be nothing.
Day in, day out—being told I am slow in understanding certain things.

Some would even make jokes that maybe I was dropped when I was a baby, so my motoring skills must have been affected. Nobody took me seriously. Everybody had an opinion of me before I could even say anything because all they would hear was my stuttering.

Each time I was told that I was only good for stuttering was a kick in the gut for me, a constant reminder of how I was a failure, how I was a mistake, and how I was not perfect. I used to cry myself to sleep every night, praying for the stuttering to go away. When I was younger, I was made to feel that my stuttering handicapped me, like a disabled person. Now, as an adult, I have learned any form of discrimination is wrong and unacceptable. Since I started to learn this as a young adult, I made sure I advocated against ableism—or discrimination against someone because of an (in)visible disability.

My stammering slowly started to go away by the time I attended university. As I got older, I found my own ways of dealing with the constant abuse and fear, and I learned how to manage my anxieties. I grew out of stammering as I felt less anxious. It did not disappear overnight, but over time I became better at handling stress and my anxiety levels. Coupled with leaving home when I did, emotional management absolutely played a positive role in providing me with some level of confidence to speak more freely.

When I had to give a talk or presentation where I had to get up in front of people, my words flowed out with no problem, like magic. The first time it happened was when I was studying for my undergrad in computer science, and at the end of the academic year, all students had to deliver presentations. My chosen topic was databases and the process called "normalisation." I initially dreaded the presentation as I was fearful of stammering, but on the actual day, I found myself in my element, and the words were flowing. I did not have to look at the script that I spent hours typing up as I ended up freestyling a lot during the fifteen-minute-long presentation.

I can't explain how happy I felt when I gave presentations. Maybe that is why, to this day, I love connecting with people through storytelling and talks. When I watched TV, I always wondered how somebody who stuttered could sing. I was a bit like that: when I had to perform in terms of delivering something, my speech would flow, but in every other circumstance, I would just make this noise and start stuttering.

Do you know what that does to one's psyche?
How it affects your mental health and well-being?
How it affects your sense of self-worth?
How it robs you of your self-respect?
How it reduces you to feeling like you are nothing?
How you are constantly reminded that you are a mistake?

My dreams, my goals, my aspirations, and what I wanted were never considered.
I could never dare to dream, to think for myself. All those choices were taken away.
I was reduced to a number and a statistic.
I was reduced to being told I was a mistake.
I kept being told I could never do anything.
I was always being told that I would never achieve anything in my life.
All because my life was not mine to plan. It was in someone's else control.
I was expected to accept my life as my fate.

But something inside me, that feisty me, always rejected the negative statements that were made about met. The way I rejected things around me was through a few ways:

- I would keep asking questions until I understood why something was presented to me as religion, when in fact, it was culture being shoved down my throat.
- I was brave and would try something I thought was right (e.g., slicing a potato in a different size and shape than what I was told to. It sounds silly, right? But that was me being defiant and challenging the status quo.)
- I would sometimes deliberately say no when asked to do something, like mopping the kitchen floor at 11:00 p.m. I was tired, my little body just needed to sleep, and I would say no, knowing very well that would mean a punishment.

In my own little ways, I was fighting and pushing boundaries at every opportunity. I just braved it, thinking I would be punished or hurt anyway, so I might as well do something that would make me feel good about myself—albeit for thirty seconds.

Something inside my heart always told me that I have to reject this, and I can never be what they want me to be. I have to be my own person. Something inside me always told me I must be more than what my family and community had wanted for me. I had this thing in me that told me I must push boundaries, I must think outside the box, and everything that I do and say is going to make everybody around me feel uncomfortable. Despite all I had to endure, all the abuses I suffered, the hardships and injustices placed upon me, I found a way to protect a certain part of myself, the part that loved myself that kept some positivity, that knew I had another destiny—a destiny in my hands. This thing inside me convinced me more that I must make others start to question their own ideologies and ways of thinking.

I knew something inside me never agreed to accept what I was being told, and I'm so grateful to God that I was built that way despite not understanding what that thing or feeling was that drove me to push past all that negativity. Whilst I was effectively being brainwashed about my life and what it meant, I knew I had to find a way to still push past all of that, so that I could have my own identity and blossom into the person who I am today—so that I could think for myself, so that I could dare to dream, so I could fight that very community that was against me. So that I could become my own person, think outside of the box, and become my own woman. I could be someone who experiences different emotions, be allowed to make mistakes, and accept those mistakes.

I'm so grateful that I had this feeling, this fire, in my belly that made me question things and be an inquisitive little girl. That drove everybody mad. It drove them so crazy that I would get smacked for questioning elders. I always kept challenging them, hence why I was labelled as the "black sheep" or "rebel" of the family.

By just being my young, inquisitive self, just asking, "Why? Why must I do this? Who said I must do that? Why did my religion tell me to do this? Whose idea was this? Surely it cannot be done in this way? What if I do not like to do it that way?" I not only annoyed everyone around me, but further classified myself as being a difficult child. I'm so grateful for being inquisitive, for questioning things. Because if I weren't, then who knows how I would have turned out?

BABA

——

My Baba was the only one in my family with whom I felt a real connection. My Baba moved to the UK—East London, to be more specific—in the 1960s. Once he was settled, he brought my mum over to join him. My eldest brother, who was ten at the time, had to be left behind with my maternal grandparents because his visa wasn't successful. This brother is my half-brother. A few years before my Baba passed away, I found out that my eldest brother's mother had passed away during labour, and Baba later married mum. My second brother was approximately three years old when my mum finally came over to join my Baba. The remaining five of us were all born and raised in London.

Baba worked a variety of roles when he came here. He was a carpenter and a labourer, and my Baba even once opened a wine bar with one of his best mates, David—or Uncle Dave, as we would call him. David was a typical East Ender, a white man who was born and raised in the heart of the East End. I have no idea how they met or became such good friends, but Baba had three best friends in total whom we grew up seeing. This group also included an Indian Hindu guy named Gogon and a fellow Bangladeshi man named Noor Ali. Growing up, it was not culturally appropriate to call an elder by their name, so we called him Uncle. It was, and still is, considered more respectful to call everyone "Uncle" or "Aunty." Uncle Noor lived with us while we were young kids, so we were closest to him.

The three of them would be in our flat on most Sundays, eating my mum's curries. Baba was a unique character. He was very different from the traditional Bangladeshi men whom I've encountered. He was very much out of the box in terms of his thinking. He did what he had to do to survive.

Baba wasn't overtly religious in his younger days—did the basics, as we say—but seeing him with his friends together having a curry at our house is a fond memory for me. I would hear them exchange stories, talk about politics or life in general, and many conversations were about food. During these conversations, I would overhear my Uncle Noor teasing Baba about how I loved him more than my own dad, as I was really attached to Uncle Noor when I was much younger. I heard stories from Uncle Noor of how I was born premature and severely underweight. I had to be placed in an incubator for a few months, and my survival was very touch and go over that period of time.

After four boys, I finally came along, and Baba used to tell me all the time how I should love, own, and embrace my name. Countless times, he told me the reason why he gave me my name was because in Arabic/Persian, Nurjahan means "bringing light into the world." He said, "I was waiting for a girl for so long, it just felt appropriate to name you that because you finally popped along and were the light into my world."

That made me feel very special and close to my Baba. It was a rare moment where, for the first time in my life, I remembered something—my name—was mine. Being the first daughter meant that was something no one could take away from me and claim as theirs.

Growing up, I saw Baba be so different from other Bangladeshi uncles, as he was not typical, and the fact that he had his own motley crew said a lot about my Baba. I was literally glued to him every time he was home. I watched him do everything and wanted to learn to do everything he did. I guess it was my way to learn and then impress my Baba. I'd want to copy him. For example, as soon as I was able to read and write, my Baba would insist that I updated his contact list.

He would do this by purchasing a new telephone/address notebook every year in January. Then he would ask me to write out the entire telephone book into the new book. It was a whole-day affair; my fingers would hurt, as I would write in my best handwriting, ensuring my writing was clear and easy for Baba to read. I would have to read aloud which name I had come across in order, and Baba would say whether I should keep that contact in or take it out of the new notebook. This made sure that the contacts were still relevant and up to date.

Baba was very organised and was militant in his organisation. I guess I learned that from him because, to this day, this is how I organise my own life. That is one of my strongest memories about Baba: how well-organised he was, how he was great at his time management, and how he was never late for anything. He always reached all his appointments thirty to sixty minutes early, just in case public transport would delay him.

I followed Baba everywhere he went, even to the post office. I used to see how he paid rent, how he paid bills, how he picked up money, and how he organised letters into folders.

We had this big old red filing cabinet where all these letters were kept and organised. It may sound like nothing, but from a young age, seeing all that discipline—like how to manage your time to update records—helped those skills come very naturally to me as I grew into an adult.

Being glued to Baba from a young age meant I learnt how to do things, such as the basics of running a house. I have memories of my Baba leaving home at dawn and coming home very late from work. He'd devote twelve or more hours a day working to make ends meet and provide for his family. I can comfortably say Baba was somebody in whom I found a lot of solace. He was my sanctuary. He was somebody who, when in the house, made me feel safe and protected. When he came home, I could finally breathe.

Baba was also traditional in many ways as he left raising the kids to mum. In my culture, mothers would be the primary teachers of all things related to rights and wrongs and how to behave. For a period of time, I think—because I was too loud, not being a typical quiet and timid kind of girl—Baba also believed I would not amount to anything.

That view did change when I would get excellent school progress reports. Teachers visited our home to convince Baba to let me attend extra classes to excel in certain areas and gave feedback on how I was doing well academically. Even though he was very pro-women's empowerment and wanted all three of his daughters to have an education, he didn't really see me going too far into higher education.

He had major aspirations for my younger sisters, as he would say my middle sister would become a doctor and my youngest sister would become a lawyer, but he never said anything about me. I think he believed I would marry young and take the hit for my sisters in that way. If the eldest daughter in a family is left "on the shelf" for too long, as the expression goes, then people will start gossiping and making assumptions that there was something wrong with me and, therefore, I was not marriage material. That would affect the family's reputation negatively and harm my younger sisters.

Mum and Baba were the first generation over here, which meant they had a lot of responsibilities. They were the first people to come abroad from their respective villages. That added a lot of pressure on my parents because now they were responsible for funding, feeding, and providing medical treatment for both sides of the family. That is a lot of pressure, and it was that pressure that forced my mother to start working as a tailor. Baba spent many years working in a coat factory in East London, and mum would tailor for the same factory where Baba worked.

My schedule for five years during high school was really intense as, in the mornings, I would have to get up and get my Baba's breakfast and lunch ready. While Baba was having his breakfast, I would begin to get lunch ready in a tiffin (a three-part stacked metal lunch container with a carry handle—like a modern-day food thermos). I would fill up his tiffin with the previous night's dinner. There would always be a vegetable curry which would become the filling for a sandwich, and that would be like an additional snack for him. I would fill up his flask with tea and then pack his bag around 6:00 a.m. Baba would take that with him when he went to work. I treasured those moments as, again, they were the few times I had with Baba that were uninterrupted.

Baba would not come home until around 8:00 to 8:30 p.m., or even 9:00 p.m., on busy nights. Mum would work literally twenty hours a day sewing. Any help I gave would support the total increase in income. I started to learn to stich on old materials and sew in a straight line. Soon after, I started to stitch along with mum so that we could make additional money and complete more quantities of the lining. The first stich I learnt was to sew in a straight line and once I mastered that then I was then in charge of sewing all the arms of the coat lining.

Both machines were in the same room, located on either side, so we had enough space to work between the beds and other furniture. This room was the middle room, which had a bunk bed, a single bed with built-in wardrobe, and two windows. Those windows were important, as they provided the room with much needed light for sewing. We used the single bed as a bench when neighbours would visit mum for a cuppa and chat. They would sit on that single bed and keep her company.

Through this experience—despite how unpleasant I found it all, despite how much I felt it was like child labour, and despite how upset I would get at being forced to work instead of playing—I learnt a lot about myself. Hindsight is wonderful. As I reflect upon these times, I can clearly see how parts of my personality developed. For example, I found out very quickly that whatever I put my mind to, I was very, very good at it, and I was a very quick learner. In fact, I worked on the machine at the speed of light. I was very good at listening and following instructions, and I discovered I was quite competitive with myself. I would always want to do better than yesterday, so I pushed myself to learn and want to do better.

I learnt a lot about textiles, sewing, and what was good or bad material. I learnt to sew blouses, shirts, skirts, trousers, and Indian clothes over time. But all of that came at a cost. It initially came at the cost of my index fingers on both hands becoming stuck where the needle pierced my fingertip through my nail on several occasions. It was a work hazard. The first time that happened, I did not initially feel anything, except the colour of my left index finger went pale and then white. I said to my mum calmly, "Mum, my finger is stuck in the needle," and my mum ran over and whacked my hand so the needle broke, and my finger was removed from the machine.

That was when it started to really hurt and bleed. I was screaming in pain. My mum sterilised a tweezer and brought it back to the room to pick out any broken needle parts she could see were stuck. Like I said, this happened several times in the first eighteen months of my sewing. Eventually, I did what my mum did each time my finger got stuck again. I would pull my own fingers away and ask mum to take the needle out of my finger.

There used to be quite a few of us living in the small three bedroom council flat—social housing—because we had relatives staying a while as a stopgap before they moved on to something else. My earliest memories were not fun, loving memories of me playing, but rather they are of me peeling ginger, garlic, onions, and potatoes. I've been cooking full time since I was nine or ten years old. Whilst I was doing all this, I had another responsibility, and that was to raise my two younger sisters. Mum was busy working all the time; therefore, I ended up doing a lot for my sisters, including clothing, feeding, and looking after them. One sister is three years younger than me, and the youngest is five years younger than me, so I ended being more of a mother to them than an older sister.

We never had the luxury of a separate dining room or dining table. We were very traditional, so we had this special type of mat. This mat was from Bangladesh, quite a handy thing as the mat was semi-heat resistant, semi-waterproof, and very easy to clean. We would place this mat on the ground and sit around in a traditional way to have our food. It was my job to make sure that I not only finished cooking in time but also to make sure dinner was ready and served on that mat by 9:30 p.m. From the moment Baba walked into the house until 9:30 p.m., Baba would wash, freshen up, perform his prayers, and then sit down to eat with us.

During the weekends, my mum could join us at lunch-time, and everyone had their own spot around this mat where they would sit. My seat was next to my Baba, and that is how I learnt how to have spicy chillies. My Baba would discreetly pass me a chilli to try with my rice and curry when mum was not looking or went back to the kitchen to top up a dish for us. Those were moments I think of fondly—I got used to having spice.

At dinner time, we would eat together as a family, except for mum, who would still be working on the machine. Mum would join us when she could. As I grew older, I learnt it was due to mum working so hard to support the wider and extended family that she gave up a lot to help others. She gave up eating with us, relaxing, and visiting her friends or our neighbours as she devoted all her time to support the family.

We had a very small, cockroach-infested kitchen, but it was a place that I had some control over, and I would clean it well. We never had cleaning products, per se, so the only things that I had to clean with were soap powder, washing up liquid, a scrub bar, and a cloth. I would get on my hands and give the floor proper elbow grease.

That's how I used to work every single day. By 11:00 p.m., I would only have either the kitchen or the bathroom as the only two remaining, uninterrupted spaces where I could use a bit of light to do some homework. But every time I would try to do that, I would get slapped and told, "Why are you wasting electricity?" I could not do my homework, so I had to go to school earlier in the morning to finish the homework that I was given the previous day.

Weekends were the worst because they just meant my days of working tirelessly were longer, with no end in sight. Weekends were distressing and very overwhelming; I was tired, being only a young kid. Our culture says that the eldest daughter, irrespective of what number you come in the pecking order, must learn all the ropes. That was just how it was done. Your responsibility was to learn to cook, to lead by example, and to be a good role model for your younger sisters. When the weekends came, I absolutely dreaded it and felt terribly sad as I could not go out and play with the other kids in the hood. If I tried to do that, I'd get slapped in the face by mum.

She was always strict with money and had to find ways to save money so it would stretch for longer. What I did was the expectations of the eldest daughter in the family—what customs and traditions demanded. It was what every girl before me had to endure. The same was expected from me. I do not feel bad for it anymore as what I went through was considered the norm, but by no means does that mean it was right. I felt my life was very restricted. I did feel my mum was stricter than most, as I saw other girls who were also the eldest in their families being allowed out and doing normal kid stuff, like playing in the park.

My desire to live better than how I lived growing up drove me to seek an education. I did not want to only have second-hand items, never being able to buy anything because I had to make a decision between eating and heating. I never had more than three sets of underwear at one time because we could never afford it.

Growing up in my culture, you're not really taught anything about puberty. You're not taught anything about how your body changes as you grow up. You're not taught about rights or wrongs in terms of behaviours and who should be around you. You're not taught anything about sex education, about healthy relationships, or anything of that kind. You have to muddle through life that way, which is incredibly unhelpful and very difficult.

In my home, every time something went wrong, I would get beaten. It always seemed to be my fault somehow. I always wondered, "Why is it that every time anything happens in the house, it's always my fault?" I wouldn't even have to be in the room—I mean, I would not even be in the house—and it was still my fault. I always ended up getting the beatings, hit with anything that was readily available, whether it was a wooden or metal spoon, a belt, or a hanger. Anything that my mum could get her hands on was used to beat me.

My Baba was oblivious to a lot of these things because he was out of the house for most of the day. If I am really honest, I guess that is why, when Baba came home, he was my sanctuary. He meant the world to me. I valued whatever time I had with my Baba. I loved it.

Baba was around a little bit more on Sundays, as he wasn't working. On Sundays, he used to get me and my brothers to do the cleaning, picking up the little hard bits stuck onto the carpet, and my brothers used to make me vacuum. We had this big, maroon-coloured showcase, and it was filled with gold and silver ornaments that Baba bought from the markets.

The showcase was a source of great pride and joy because it cost a lot of money. Baba would go to the market and pick up different ornaments, and then, he would bring them in and put them on the glass shelves. We had to clean these ornaments with this product that felt like wet tissues. We would rub the ornaments, which were different animals and birds, and make them shiny. Baba loved collecting them.

I would have to spend time after that cleaning all the dust off the shelves, wiping them down, and folding the prayer mats into one of the corners of the showcase. The bottom part of the showcase had the cupboards, which held all of our crockery, fancy dinnerware, and glass sets. These were only accessible when we had guests over, so they were for special people.

Friday was a big day, not only for religious reasons but also because it was payday. Baba did the big weekly shop on Friday. Usually, my youngest brother, Imran, would go shopping with Baba to a particular grocery shop and spend between fifty and sixty pounds—a lot of money to spend on a food shop in the 1980s. There were two things that my parents never were tight on: food and heating. I remember that Imran would feel important for being the one who supported Baba in the shop, and he enjoyed the two pounds' taxi ride back home. Imran even used to do his best to man up and carry all the shopping bags from the taxi up one flight of stairs.

Saturday nights were a great way for all of us siblings to get together and spend time with Baba. He would rent a couple of Bollywood movies; it was VHS player and cassettes back in those days. I would sit with Baba, and my siblings would join. Together, we'd watch a marathon of two or three movies. I guess it was Baba's own way of relaxing and resting. The funny thing was he would be up again on Sunday morning to go to the market. On most Sunday afternoons, Baba would cook a few curries; his specialty was cooking chicken in two ways. The first curry would be on its own, and the second curry would be with a vegetable.

I loved skipping along behind my Baba in the mornings at the Sunday market. He would wake us up early in the morning on Sunday to get there before all the good items were gone. We used to walk down this entrance of the market, and there would be this burger van, and man, the smell was just amazing!

Even now, when I smell that, it takes me right back to those Sunday mornings.

Once Imran asked Baba why he cooked on his only day off in the week; Baba responded that every man should learn how to cook in case he needs to feed his family especially, if mum was unwell. I have grown up seeing my Baba cook, and he taught me how to cook. It was from those early days that Baba made sure all the boys in our family learnt how to cook and demonstrated the importance of survival skills. My Baba was a very good cook, by the way, and he taught my mum how to cook.

On those Sunday mornings, Baba would go to wake my brothers up at 6:00 a.m. (they all slept in the same room) and the elder two would always pretend to be in a deep sleep. So, when Baba would push their shoulders to wake-up, they would act like they were fast asleep. Imran was the lighter sleeper, so when Baba woke him, he would just jump out of bed. Most of the time, he would be the one to go with Baba to the market. As Baba walked fast, we had to run to be able to catch up with him. I used to hold Baba's hand as much as possible so I would not lose the pace.

There were two markets on that particular stretch of road, so once we visited the first market, we would walk to the next one, where Baba would typically meet with Uncle Noor.

Sometimes Uncle Noor would part ways with us at the bus stop, but most of the time, he would grab the bus back home with us and stay at our flat for the rest of the day and Uncle Dave and Uncle Gogon would come over.

On the days I would be lucky enough to go with them, I loved how Baba would visit literally every single stall—how he used to love buying bananas. I think I may have inherited my Baba's bargaining skills, as he used to haggle for absolutely everything. If the stall owners screamed "Two pounds for a bag of bananas!" Baba would say, "I will give you fifty pence." Baba's incredibly low-price offers used to make me laugh; he was a no-nonsense sort of man, and he did not waste time.

My favourite part of the Sunday market was going to the penny sweet store. Baba would buy us these bags of sweets as treats when we were with him, and they were special because they were not something we had very often. We could almost never afford them, so they were a luxury item for us.

While writing this book, I shared stories with my siblings, and when it came to Baba, we remembered his ability to look a lot younger than he was and his love for being trendy. I have vague memories of Baba visiting the clothing stalls in these markets, looking for the perfect blazer and pair of trousers. He had an eye for detail and had creams and oils to take care of his beard, hair, and face. His outward appearance matched his heart.

Having that shared community was very much central to our culture and a common practice for us. On top of that, our home was always popular as everyone came to our flat, and we were the main hub. I used to wonder why we had so many visitors, but now I realise that everyone loved spending time with my parents. We would go to our neighbour's house when the opportunity allowed us, and the kids would run in and out of each other's homes freely. I saw my Baba sharing whatever we had with guests, and I really loved that about my culture.

Gathering at our flat was such a great way to get together. That's something we do not have anymore. My Baba was a very giving person. He had a very big heart. If we had just one bowl of rice, he would give that to the guests who were in our home at mealtime. When you grow up seeing that, you can't help but develop into that kind of person, because my Baba would emphasise the importance of sharing what you have. He would tell us that sharing what you have never diminished from your wealth in any way. In fact, he said you will be blessed with so much more—meaning you never lose when you share with others.

My Baba used to do a lot of community work. He used to always support women—both within our immediate community and the wider world—who were going through difficulties. For example, if they were experiencing domestic abuse, he would take them down to the women's shelter or help them fill out paperwork. My Baba was one of few people around who could read, write, and speak English. He was always the one filling out forms until I got to the stage where I could read and write. He used to make me practice all the time, and I used to accompany my Baba on different visits.

My Baba supported those who were in need in a variety of different ways. These included accompanying them to the police station or social services and dropping women off at the women's shelters. He filled out forms, spoke over the phone to different organisations, and physically gave away items we had in our house to help those in need and who were trying to leave their abusers. Baba would give them crockery, our blankets, bedsheets, pillows, and even clothes.

I grew up seeing all of that, but I also saw a lot of the community not approving of what my Baba used to do because he was going against the cultural norms, where abuse was often tolerated and brushed under the carpet. Baba's actions caused a lot of tension within some parts of the community, and many men did not understand why my Baba would do something that was so out there. Baba was a great pillar in the community; he was a change maker and definitely a trailblazer.

I grew up inheriting many of Baba's qualities, such as his stubbornness, and many people tell me that my personality resembles Baba's so much. It's quite amazing when I think back on many of the activities in which I am involved in are because they are always about helping, uplifting, and empowering those who are vulnerable and less fortunate than me. I too have done and continue to do things that my community absolutely hates. They think I am corrupting girls by sharing and supporting young women's rights to stand up for themselves and take charge of their lives.

It's no wonder that I have become the person I am—that I want to give back to others and serve the most vulnerable in our society. I have witnessed so much hardship that women had to experience because they had no family, could not speak English, or had no education, no career, and no way to be independent. Since I saw Baba helping such women, I guess it was only a matter of time before I would follow in similar footsteps. I'm like a duplicate of my Baba in terms of appearance, character, and personality, and growing up, seeing Baba do so much had a huge role in developing me into who I am today.

I strongly believe that my desire to help those who are in need, who are vulnerable, or less fortunate than myself, stems from those years of seeing how my Baba used to give hope to others. I had become my Baba's caregiver in the last six or seven years of his life, when he suffered a series of strokes and heart attacks. As his caregiver, I looked after him, fed him, and supported him in his everyday activities. After he had his third heart attack, he became wheelchair bound. He was lucky to come back home as the doctors at that time said he would not last more than a few days, but he lived for another sixteen months. During those last sixteen months of his life, I became a full-time caregiver. I would move him from the commode to the bed and from the bed to the sofa, and I was the one injecting his insulin as he was scared of needles.

During this period of time, when Baba was in a wheelchair, we managed to visit the factory Baba used to work in where he was a coat presser. If Baba ever had to pick up something or drop something off, we would pop in. I remember how much everyone around him both in and out of work respected him. Everyone greeted my Baba as he walked on the streets, like everyone knew him. Everyone would come to Baba for advice, filling out even more forms, reading and translating letters, and always being there for people.

Imran and I were probably the closest to Baba, and Imran is the brother to whom I am closest. He is only two years older than me, so our ages are similar. We did a lot for Baba in the last sixteen months of his life. Imran spent more time with Baba after his third heart attack, as it was he who wheeled Baba to shops regularly. I think the reality that Baba would not always be here started to kick in for Imran when we almost lost him that time, so when Baba did come home, we knew how lucky we were that our father had survived.

When Baba moved into the front room, he slept on the sofa bed during the daytime, and Imran would lay down next to him to talk and keep him company. Baba had daily visitors, that showed us how popular he was. Even whilst Baba was so sick, he would still teach us elements of our faith. For example, Baba showed so much gratitude when anyone visited him and he explained to me and Imran how our faith rewarded those who visited the sick.

When Baba passed away, I was sixteen. I was one of three people in the family—Imran and my mother being the other two—who witnessed my Baba passing away. Despite the highs and lows, my parents still had a very loving relationship. My Baba would talk to my mum in his Bollywood style, saying, "When I die, I want to die in your arms." He said that often, and as kids, we used to laugh when we heard that as open displays of affection were not something common in our culture. But that's exactly how my Baba passed away in the end; my Baba died in my mum's arms while she fed him grapes in the hospital.

When he died, my mum screamed. The doctors had said that when my Baba passes away, they would not resuscitate him because he would only come back in a vegetative state. Everybody had come to see my Baba to pay their last respects and say their goodbyes. It was the most bizarre feeling, watching my Baba die in front of me. I stood at the top of the bed, looking at him while all the commotion was taking place. Doctors and nurses came running into the cubicle and eventually declared him dead.

Mum freaked out and started screaming. One of my uncles had to come and take her away. The rest of the family was waiting down the hall in the waiting room. I just stood there watching all of this going in what felt like slow motion right in front of me. I just froze. I thought, *Oh my God, this is it.* My Baba's gone. The one person I care about, the one person who cared about me, is now gone.

I used to spend time with Baba at the hospital, and Imran and I rotated being there each day. Between us and mum, we would stay with him and never left him alone. I would spend time reciting our holy book to him or with him. I did everything I could to make him as comfortable as possible. He would often tell visitors who came to see him, "My daughter, she's the best. She's never left my side. She is always making me feel better or rubbing my back, feeding me, wiping me, and putting a smile on my face."

When Baba had his third heart attack, the doctors gave him three days to live, but he lived on for sixteen more months. So, when he had this fourth heart attack, I was hopeful that he would come back home again. I mean, the doctors had said he would not make it last time, but he did. As Baba took his last breath, Uncle Noor was there praying, straightening his arms, his legs, and taking my father's dentures out of his mouth. And then he pulled the bedsheet over Baba's face.

I felt like I was choking. I couldn't breathe. I felt paralysed—I just could not believe what was happening in front of me. In a zombie-like fashion, I slowly walked over to Baba and removed the bedsheet. My Baba looked so happy. He was smiling. He looked at peace. I remember kissing my Baba's forehead and cheek, and I started to cry. Uncle Noor consoled me and covered Baba's face once more.

I started to walk back to the waiting room to tell my sisters, but obviously they had seen all the commotion with mum. Everybody had to witness my mum screaming. My two sisters came running towards me, and both grabbed me around my waist, crying and asking if Baba had died. I started to cry. I mean, what could I have said to my sisters, who were so young? My sisters' hearts were broken, witnessing mum breaking down the way she did. They were absolutely terrified.

As my sisters became distraught by all the commotion, I couldn't cry anymore. I had these two little girls crying for their Baba. The three of us sat together in the waiting room until we left for home that evening. Everything else after that happened so quickly. The funeral would take place the following day. In our culture, you bury immediately, and I remember everybody had asked me, "Do you want to go see your Baba again?" For some reason, I got really scared to go see my Baba and said no.

But I wish I had. I wish I had the courage to have seen him one more time, but I didn't go see my Baba. That has been my biggest regret to this day. The only time I got to see my Baba again was at the mosque, where I only got to see his face through the little glass panel that was above his face on the coffin. I couldn't touch him. I could not have any alone time with him to say my own goodbye.

He looked so beautiful. He looked so at peace, and I remember screaming and saying, "He's smiling!" There's no way he could be dead. He just looked so at peace.

The days and weeks after that were horrendous because life was just a big blur. I had to take charge of everything. I had to organise who was making food. So many people came and went, so I had to organise drinks for them. My mum was in a complete state of shock and eventually went into clinical depression. Everybody kept telling me, a little sixteen-year-old girl, to stay strong for my family.

I mean, what the hell was I supposed to do? Why did I all of a sudden have to become the pillar and be strong for the entire family?

On the second day, I sat down in a corner of one of the rooms crying, trying to begin my grieving process for Baba. One of the aunties screamed at me, asking me why I was crying. She violently grabbed my arms and dragged me up so I was standing and then shook my shoulders, all the while saying, "Now is not the time to cry!" I could feel her spit and bits of betel nut that she had been chewing fall on my face. She then slapped me across my face and shook me violently by my shoulders, saying, "Why are you crying? You need to man up."

So now I needed to man up? *Now* it was okay for me to be the man and not any other time? Now I had to man up and take charge and look after the family. I had these dark red marks on my face that dried up, something I noticed when I went to the bathroom afterwards to wash my face with water.

Since that day, I have not cried nor grieved for my Baba. It's now been twenty-four years since he passed away, and the way that aunty treated me has left me traumatised to this day.

I still have not grieved for my Baba's death as in the back of my head he's still in the hospital. It sounds really messed up; I know. But that's how I deal with my Baba's death. If I didn't feel that he was still around, then I would feel my entire world would collapse in a split second. Since the day Baba died, I no longer felt safe and protected.

I no longer had a sanctuary.
I no longer had anyone to care for and love me.
I no longer had somebody to look up to.

I no longer had somebody to tell me everything would
be okay.
I no longer had somebody to touch my head and tell me
that I would get better.
I no longer had somebody come into my room when I was
stressing about school.
I no longer had somebody to kiss my forehead and tell me
everything would be fine.

Everything I do is with the intention that it makes my
Baba happy and for my Baba to be proud of me. Everything
that I have achieved today I have done with the drive that it
would have made my Baba happy.

My Baba is the reason why I do most things. All the
things that he used to say hit me at different times in my
life because they have started to make sense as I continue to
grow and develop.

HOMELESS

———

I had just stepped off the N15 night bus and found myself in Piccadilly Circus, and as soon as my foot touched the ground, that was the beginning of a journey that would see me desperately striving to survive and carve out a space for myself amongst the homeless community—a space that you had to fight for and a necessity to stay alive.

I was wearing a warm fleece and my Dr. Martens boots that night as it was cold and rainy, and I felt the drop in temperature. I sat on a bus seat that had heating underneath it and spent a few hours on that bus as it went along its night route. The windows were steamed from the rain outside, and I could see the different lights as it weaved through the streets of London.

It was 1998 when I decided to attend university. Tony Blair had just come into power and abolished grants for higher education, leaving me with no means of paying my tuition fees. I was nineteen years old, and university was unheard of at the time in my community. Neither my brothers nor any of the young boys in my neighbourhood had gone into higher education—let alone any of the girls.

After the first few months of university, I started to really understand how going against the wishes of my family and the wider community was grating them; everyone had a problem with me doing something that was unheard of at that time. At first when I attended classes at university, I made excuses and lied to my family about where I was going. However, as I was attending regularly, and it took a while to travel to class, those around me started to notice a pattern.

They asked more direct questions about where I was going, and I had to admit I was attending university. That did not land well with anyone. This led to a lot of arguments—my family would try to exert control and power over me, telling me to stop attending university, as it was a waste of time. They, along with the neighbours and the wider community, would question why I would "waste" years studying when I would just end up being a housewife, having to cook, clean, and breed.

Things at home became even more difficult as my family would physically lock me in the house so I could not leave home and go to university. Over those months, I endured physical, verbal, and mental abuse. I kept repeating myself, trying to explain why education was so important to me. I kept telling them I wanted to be my own person, that I wanted to learn, I wanted to experience what it felt like to inform my own opinions, how education would benefit not only me but the future generations, and it was my right to learn.

Each time I would shout out these responses, someone would strike me. Sometimes I would feel a hand slap my face, or an elbow hitting my head, or a foot kicking me in my gut. Other times, they would use tools to exert even more power over me—an attempt to slowly and completely break me. One day, it could be a metal hanger, a belt, a hammer, or a metal rod hitting my body in an attempt to silence me. All the while

I would experience this abuse, I would scream even louder, saying, "I will go to university whether you like it or not!"

The weird part of all this abuse was that it did not actually deter me; it actually made me even more determined to study. The more they attempted to break my body—break my spirit—the more I told myself that when I get out of this situation, I will show them what I can achieve.

One day, things escalated when I got caught managing to slip out to go to university. That night, I came home knowing very well that I would suffer the consequences of my actions. I knew it would be bad, so I was both scared and determined at the same time. That night, it went from bad to worse when my (at that time, substance-addicted) brother attempted to stab me in my shoulder, which forced me to leave home. He gave me a very good flesh wound. I managed to fill a bag of key items and left home with the intention to never return. When I did that, all hell broke loose, as in my community there are only two ways a young girl leaves her father's home: marriage or death.

I managed to secure accommodation on campus and continued two of the four jobs that I had. I really struggled to keep up with rent as I was earning nowhere near enough to put a roof over my head, feed me, and clothe me. Very soon, I found myself in a position where I could no longer afford to pay rent. I was then evicted, but I felt too embarrassed to go to any of my Muslim friends. There was no way I was going back home. Being the young, feisty woman, I was also too proud to ask for direct help. I didn't want people from my community to judge me or say things that I had already heard from my family.

When I first became homeless and was sofa surfing, I had to swallow my pride and start asking my non-Muslim friends if I could stay with them "for a few days" while I arranged alternative, longer-term accommodation, knowing very well that I had no other options and no idea how I would make alternative arrangements. I would lie on these sofas at night, never really able to sleep because I had this heavy feeling in my heart, wondering what I was going to do next. Who else could I ask for a favour? I had a hundred and one questions run through my mind as I thought about who I could ask for help, and that was a very difficult thing for me to do—asking for help.

The guilt I felt eventually made me hop from one friend's place to another for almost three months. Where I outstayed my welcome, I broke meaningful friendships and very soon found myself being on the N15 night bus and then in Piccadilly Circus. I would often think, "What kind of life do I have where, by day, I'm a student and, at night, I'm homeless?"

I soon ran out of friends to ask—out of options. I was left with no choice but to start knocking on the doors of institutions, organisations, and fellow Muslims to ask for help.

That first time I knocked on a door to ask for help, I had to spend the entire afternoon plucking up the courage to not feel embarrassed. It felt like I was begging, and I was worried about what they would think of me. I did not want to be made to feel any worse because I was already at my lowest point. After praying, reciting a few religious texts, I straightened myself up, tried to look as presentable as possible, and walked up to an organisation's door. I had rehearsed in my head so many times what I would say and kept changing it up so I would not sound like I was desperate. With the first door I knocked on, my palms were sweating, my hands were shaking, and my voice was breaking as I tried to explain my situation and land the message that I really needed some help.

I was expecting to be helped, to be taken in and looked after. I genuinely did not believe that I would not be helped. However, the moment I heard the organisation say to me that they did not want to help me, did not want to get involved, that they were supposedly not in a position to help me, those words broke me. All the abuse I had suffered could not break me or my spirit, but those words—the way they turned me away, the way the door slammed shut in my face—did.

I froze for what felt like forever. I could not move, could not speak, could not believe my ears. Tears were rolling down my face as I tried to make sense of what had just happened. I refused to believe that the beauty of my own community, the one I had been born into and the one that Baba said was the best of mankind, did not exist. I struggled to reconcile my personal experience and what I had grown up hearing and seeing through my Baba. I grew up believing that we are a group of people who always help those in need, that we help those who are less fortunate than us, and, no matter what, we look after the women in our community.

I was taught that my community was kind, gentle, loving, caring, and helpful to everyone in need, like my Baba was with every person he had helped—like my Baba was with every woman he took out of a dangerous environment and supported to seek help. I was always taught that this community of mine would help you at your time of need, that they want for you what they want for themselves. As the tears started to stream down my face, I wiped them away, and I knocked again on that same door. I had this sudden adrenaline rush to demand answers. I did not care what they might think of me.

I asked them, "Why won't you help me?" I asked, "Where is your compassion?" I asked, "Where am I supposed to get help if you don't help me?" They directed me to a church who served hot meals and provided shelter in their church hall during the cold winter months that we were in. I must admit it took me years to get over that first incident, took me years to accept what had happened to me. Still, I continued knocking on doors when I needed help.

So, I knocked on the next set of doors, and this time, I was made to feel that the situation was my fault, that as a female Muslim I should be ashamed of myself for ruining my family's reputation, dishonouring them, and for leaving home in the first place. They screamed at me with abusive language, and I was told that I deserved to be in this situation.

I stopped as I could no longer take the constant judgement, the constant insults hurled at me and being told I should be ashamed for putting myself in this situation—as though it was out of choice or for fun. What my community did to me without even realising added to my already heavy shoulders.

They added to my already broken heart. They added to my already lacking sense of self-worth.

For a number of years, they drove me to believe my community was evil. They did not uphold the very essence of what my faith taught me—what my Baba taught me—which was to love for your brother what you love for yourself, to be gentle and kind, and to help those who are vulnerable and less fortunate than yourself. This was a time when I had hit rock bottom.

The overwhelming feeling that no one wanted me, no one loved me, no one would look after me, no one wanted to help me, convinced me more that I was a burden. I did not deserve anything good to happen to me. After a few months of no longer seeing the point of being here, I attempted suicide, as I could not take the pain anymore. I felt that being dead was better than living a life where I was constantly told I was at fault.

During this period of my life, I lived out of my infamous rucksack and three bin liners, which held any possessions of importance. My rucksack was well-known by my friends and peers, as I had everything that anyone could ever want in that bag, similar to how women often seem to have endless items in their handbags. During my university days I got along with almost everyone and anybody, and my good relations with the security guys meant I was able to store my three bin liners in the cleaning storage area.

My routine was supported by the fact that I would go into university as soon as the doors would opened around 7:00 a.m. and use that time in the morning to say hello to a range of staff (security, library, canteen, and academics) and forget my problems for a few moments. I would be there from morning until late into the evening, when they closed the library.

By doing this, I projected an image of being very studious, but the reality was far from that. I would stay at the university for as long as physically possible so I could be safe and warm. This was compounded even further by the fact that I felt I could not share my troubles with anybody. I coped and accepted my life on the streets. I would stay awake for most of the night, too scared to sleep in case something happened to me. I saw many girls and women attacked, assaulted, raped, and beaten whilst being on the streets. Even now, I still suffer from sleep issues because of that lingering fear. Being all alone on the streets was a dark place.

Unfortunately, whilst I was homeless, I saw and heard far too much. When I reflect back on those days, I remember how each night felt like an eternity. I never imagined I would be on the streets for as long as I was. Each passing night turned into weeks and then into months. As time passed, I became more exposed to the harsh and cruel world for those who are part of the homeless community. It became apparent very quickly how women are the most vulnerable group within the homeless population and just how much risk women are exposed to.

One of the most emotionally and mentally challenging aspects of homelessness was learning how society and the public are quick to make judgements about you because they see you on the street and make assumptions without understanding or wanting to understand how your situation may have come about. People are unwilling to understand that, more often than not, those experiencing homelessness are stuck between a rock and a hard place.

People don't choose this way of life.
People don't wake-up one morning and decide, "Okay, I'm going to be homeless today."

Individual circumstances force many individuals to go to the streets. Sometimes being on the streets is safer than being in a more harmful environment. Some may need to leave an abusive home and therefore have no choice but to leave what they knew.

Then, you have people like me who, despite having family and a supposed community around me, were rejected, pushed away, and alienated all because they wanted to pursue an education. You have people like me who are forced into living on the streets just because they wanted something more from life.

And why?

All because I had hope.
All because I believed.
All because I deserved better.
All because I did not want to be yet another statistic who became a mother and a wife.
All because I believed there are multiple roles for women.
All because I believed in myself.

Nobody knows my journey. Nobody understood. Nobody—neither my friends, my peers, nor my family—can ever understand what I went through. They can't understand, and they won't be able to understand, as in their eyes, I had a choice not to be homeless.

I would not wish anybody to be homeless.
I would not wish anybody to lick KFC bones.
I would not want anyone to rummage through public bins to find leftover food to eat because you are literally starving.
I would not want anyone to feel those hunger pangs in their stomach because they have not eaten for four consecutive nights.
I would not want anyone to make the horrid choice between food or tampons.
I would not want anyone to experience what I have, because it cripples you.
It cripples you physically as you are limited in what you can do due to fear of being attacked.
It cripples you emotionally as you are in a constant state of anxiety.
It cripples you mentally as your sense of self-worth, dignity, and self-respect goes down the pan.

When you have all these troubles crippling you with zero support, it becomes impossible to pick yourself up. It becomes impossible to see light at the end of the tunnel. I had to dig deep to find some hope to pull through this experience.

When you see somebody on the streets, all they want is for you to talk to them, as that world is lonely. A simple "Hello" goes a long way and asking someone how their day has been can be the one thing that brings a smile to their face.

It is lonely being homeless. It is lonely not having anybody talk to you. It is lonely trying to figure things out for yourself. It is lonely trying to work out what you should or shouldn't do. Nobody knew the full truth, that behind the image of the studious young woman, I was losing friends and having doors shut in my face. This all added to my loneliness, my isolation, and my wanting to end my life.

LOVE OF LEARNING

———

Education has always been important to me. What started out as a form of escapism eventually turned into a passion, a love of learning, and a way of bettering myself. Academia became important to me because, from a young age, I never heard or saw anybody talk about education as something positive. I grew up in an environment where education was never a priority and was a means to an end to get through high school as that would be enough to be able to speak and write basic English and get by in life.

Despite everything and everyone around me thinking education was a huge no, I always knew from a young age that the only way to change my life was through school. As a result, I became determined not to let myself become that statistic—being yet another woman marrying at a young age and having kids. Every time someone screamed at me, called me "Owah," or told me I was good for nothing, this little voice in my head would respond, "Just wait; I will show you all."

That determination, that drive, that fire in my belly kept growing, and after college I was itching to prove to everyone around me and to the world that I would become something. That I would amount to something. That I would have my own voice. That I would bring benefit to others. I would show everyone the true value of education and how it can be beneficial not only to me as the one directly learning but also as a means to uplift others around me, especially other women.

Growing up, the women in my community were in one of two camps. The first camp was those who understood the game. These women learnt through their early experiences when to keep their mouths shut, not question anything, and get their needs met through being bought things and finding small pleasures in life. These were women who had come over to the UK via their spouses, married quite young, and had a few children. They adapted to this life, fully understanding their limitations but also looking to maximise in the areas where they did have some control. For example, they might have spent all of their time shopping, finding materialistic pleasures in life.

The second camp were women who also came to the UK via their spouses but failed miserably to fully adjust. They were oppressed, not clever enough to work out the game they needed to play. Due to not having any family or a support network, they had no other choice but to accept this life. Both types of women could be found in my neighbourhood. Both types of women suffered and accepted a limited life.

These two camps bred another generation of women who would grow up seeing women in these two camps, and the cycle would continue. I saw a lot of this as the block of flats we lived in had twenty-four homes across four floors, all of which, minus a few, were Bangladeshi families. That meant that I saw many women who were either growing up like me, going through something similar, or women who were brought to the UK on spouse visas and were silenced into conformity to their husband's family's norm and traditions.

As we lived on the first floor, there were five other flats on the same floor. Out of those five flats, I grew up witnessing two families in particular where the women married into the family from abroad and had a difficult life. These women were not accepted, as they were considered outsiders. The son's behaviour was viewed to have changed since the new wife came on the scene, or the new wife/daughter-in-law was seen as not adjusting well.

I saw this production line of women leaving everything they knew and moving to a new country, not knowing the language or its way of life. The way they were treated can only be described as these women becoming slaves to these families. They only ever cooked, cleaned, and bore children. Each woman was either spoken ill of all the time and publicly humiliated at every given opportunity, or her parents would be cursed if she made a mistake in fulfilling a chore. I naturally felt akin to such women, and I would speak with them and joke around with them as much as I could to help them feel better. I knew only too well how they felt.

I always wondered why there could not be a third camp. Where young girls could dream, could hope, could believe they could become something in life.

As I grew older, I kept learning and re-learning how anti-education everyone was through a number of ways. These included young girls being discouraged from becoming something when they grew older, or by being surrounded by a language that was always negative about women in general. Or they were always hearing how, by default, a woman's role was to get married as soon as possible and have their own family.

Adults in the community put a lot of emphasis on ensuring that girls learnt all the "relevant" skills to make her future in-laws proud. Could she cook all the different varieties of dishes? Could she bake? Could she sew and be handy around the house? Could she clean properly, and did she have an eye for detail for interior design? What I have described is and was very common within many cultures around the world, so I guess my own culture was no different.

There was no vision for these girls to go into any kind of profession.

Each time I heard the negativity, my love for education only grew and the idea that education was my only escape route further cemented in my mind and heart.

You know that green exit sign you see hanging over fire escape doors? That was my image of this escape route. I always viewed myself running through the exit. I somehow knew that education would allow me to make choices for myself, to see how others lived their lives, and to hear other people's opinions. It would give me the opportunity to develop and formulate my own ideas, my own concepts, in life. I understood from a very young age that if I could excel in education, then that would be my ticket out of an environment that had concluded I was a waste of space.

Every day we made tough choices; all of those around me were doing their best to survive, and perhaps we needed to be focused on thriving. My community, restricted by the ideals of the past, continued to perpetuate these ideals, perhaps guised by the view of supporting one another.

So, when I thought of university, it felt like a distant dream. It genuinely felt like something that was impossible for common people. I always thought that if somebody went to university, they must be from an affluent background, have contacts in high places, and be privileged. During the time I attended university, there was no one else in my neighbourhood who was going. When I was a young girl, I would never in a million years have imagined that I, Nurjahan Khatun from Tower Hamlets, who grew up in relative poverty, would ever go to university, let alone attain two degrees.

It was absolutely unheard of that a woman from my community could, or would even dare to, attend university. It was not the norm in any way, and I believe that I was probably one of the first females in my community to go to university. There were certainly many cultural barriers, and my father was the only one who had supported my education. He was the only one who was pro-education for women.

When I left home at nineteen to study, I went through a time when my family rejected me. I struggled financially, and that led to my homelessness. Once I got back on my feet, post-homelessness, I was able to go on to complete my second degree. After I had finally graduated with my masters, I returned home for my two younger sisters; they had been asking me for such a long time to come back. I felt more like a mother to them than a sister, so I decided to return. I knew that coming back would be hard, if not impossible, for me. I had to tread carefully and think, "How can I escape this life in a way that doesn't impact my sisters?" This way, my younger sisters would have a better chance of receiving good marriage proposals.

I figured out that education was most probably my only exit route out of a life that I feared living—a woman whose only purpose was to be someone's wife and someone's mother. I refused to only have meaning in life through a husband. I was adamant to avoid getting stuck in the same environment forever. I did not want to be miserable, unhappy, and feel like a lonely woman whose sole purpose was to serve everyone except herself.

Looking back, I do wonder how the hell a young kid who had almost zero positive exposure (except from Baba) learnt that self-love and self-care started with herself, but something inside me knew that I had to do what would make me happy and get at least part of what I wanted.

It's actually quite remarkable just how powerful this feeling was, how it gave me hope and strength—strength to put up with all the constant abuse, strength to be able to look forward to a new day as I chose to believe that something would change. Even on days when I felt nothing would ever change. I really cannot explain how I found the strength to dig deep enough to be cheerful, always smiling and remain positive. As a child, I was always laughing, showing off my dimples, advertising my big white teeth, and showing the biggest heart, helping others whenever I was given the opportunity to do so.

The narrative of women and education did change once I pushed those barriers, as I had paved the way for my younger sisters to pursue education should they want to. My younger sisters did not have to endure what I did, as I had taken the hit for them and many other young girls in the neighbourhood. My attending university sparked a conversation in the community about the role of young girls: could they add value to families and the wider community? Could the family reap the benefits of a girl's education once she made a career for herself? So, after I had gone to university, the tone and language of the conversation went from, "You cannot attend university," to "Why don't you want to go to university?"

I used to hear my Baba say to my mum how he wanted all his girls to attain an education so we always had something to lean back on should we ever need it and he wasn't really worried about the boys as boys can survive in this world.

Quite often my mum would argue and say, "Education won't get girls far," or "It's not for girls." What's the point of getting degrees when, in a roundabout way, a girl is going to end up having to be a homemaker, wife, and mother?

It is interesting how the eldest daughter—irrespective of which number sibling they are in the overall order—shoulders so much burden. Although I was fifth out of seven siblings, I was the eldest out of the girls, so that meant I had to be a role model to my two younger sisters. I was told all the time that the way I dressed, talked, behaved, and guarded my honour would reflect positively or negatively on my sisters. If I misbehaved and turned out "wrong," then my sisters would have a bad role model, and the chances of them ending up like me would be high. If I did any wrong, then my sisters would copy me, thinking it was okay to do because I did it.

I could not be a child and make mistakes because if I did, then I would get a beating or a telling off. I always had to be aware of what I was doing and saying, in case I would be punished and told that I was a bad influence on my sisters. I never quite understood why all the responsibility for how my two younger sisters would turn out was on my head. I never quite understood why I had to shoulder that burden. How could a child be responsible for such a thing that I had no control over?

My mother married very young, and that left her with, in my opinion, a very narrow-minded view of the world. She was very traditional. My Baba was a lot older than her, and he had seen a lot of the world for himself in order to formulate opinions that were very much pro-woman compared to those of his peers. My mother was a great believer in tradition and how the role of women was very specific and defined.

In her world, a woman married, had children, and became a homemaker.

My Baba was very much pro-education, and because of him, I had the energy, the courage, the audacity to think that I could attend university. My Baba supported me in a way that he didn't fully realise. When he passed away, I was only sixteen, and that loss felt like my only support for further education was also gone. I pushed through during this difficult period and managed to complete college; by this time, I was incredibly determined that I wanted to attend university.

Everyone had benefited from free education, and now that I wanted to attend, that chance felt like it was taken away from me. I had to somehow try to pull together £1,300, so I asked a couple of my neighbours around our home, and they all came one by one into the front room.

I had spent a few hours before then cleaning up the front room. I had cleaned and dusted the showcase, which was dark red in colour, and I used the cloth and warm water to clean the inside of the glass cabinets, wiping away the dust particles. I used the shiner that my Baba used to clean all the silver ornaments from the market. I tidied up the cushions on the sofa beds, hoovered, and sprayed enough air freshener to knock any person out. I patted out the mustard-coloured curtain, wiped down the white-painted windowsills, and refolded the prayer mats and left them on the corner coffee table. I finally made sure all the white thrills of the red rug that were in the centre of the front room were straightened out

I wanted to give the best impression possible before doing the most difficult thing I'd ever done in my eighteen years of life.

Half a dozen individuals came into the front room, and I said I wanted to speak to them. The look on their faces read, "What the hell am I doing here?" Because I was so nervous, I had made some notes on a kitchen towel so I wouldn't forget what I needed to ask. I straightened out my clothes and made sure all my hair was covered. I tried to make sure my look and demeanour screamed capable yet innocent. I did not want to come across as the feisty girl I was known for, and I did not want to come across as the dumb and loud one— rather, someone who was confident but not too confident. I had to be believable, yet vulnerable.

As it was the first time students would need to pay tuition fees, and I wasn't eligible for any funding, I decided to do something quite creative, asking my neighbours if I could borrow some money to pay for my first year tuition fees. I used my notes written on the kitchen towel and gave a five-minute speech in front of these elders, who I regarded quite highly. I had to show them respect because of age.

I started by announcing my aspiration to attend university and that I needed financial support. I went on to say that I had invited them over to ask if they would lend me a couple hundred pounds each, as that would allow me to pay for the fees. I outlined how I had every intention of returning the money as soon as I could post-graduation.

Their reaction was heart-wrenching. They stood up and laughed at me, saying,
- "Why are you trying to wear the trousers of the house?"
- "Do you think you're a man?"
- "Why do you think you could go to university?"

My little heart broke into a million pieces, and I ran out of the room crying. I spent the next few days continuing to cry.

Everyone in my family was dealing with the death of my Baba in their own way; my brothers were never home, my mum was becoming clinically depressed, and my younger sisters were too young to even understand what was going on. So, I decided to take a gap year and earn the money myself. I would work and save so I could pay my tuition fees the following year. I had never worked in my life, never ventured out to the big bad world—as I had lived in this protective bubble up until then.

Work is exactly what I did, and in that gap year, I worked four jobs. I managed to get a job with a bank, and I worked full-time Monday to Friday. I spent two hours in the early morning and two hours in the evening cleaning toilets and offices. Thursday and Friday nights, I worked at a hotel as a night reception in West London. Then, all-day Saturday and all-day Sunday, I worked fourteen-hour shifts. I worked in the local supermarket called Cost Cutter in East London. I was literally working seven days a week nonstop. And in the tenth month, I collapsed from exhaustion and was hospitalised for a couple of weeks.

It was a horrendous time because I was not only working but also, as soon as I got home, I would have to do the cooking and the chores. Mum was clinically depressed and getting mum to the bathroom was virtually impossible, so I had to become the adult and the mother very quickly—not only for myself and my mother but also for my two younger sisters. I remember I would instruct my younger sisters to get all the preparations ready, because the moment I sat down, I was unable to get back up. As soon as I walked through the front door, I would head directly for the kitchen and cook and get that out of the way. My sisters would help me do a bit of cleaning, but that is how I managed that gap year while taking care of my responsibilities towards my family and pursing my dreams.

During my gap year, I was the one that lifted the mantle and took care of my family. The government changed the system for benefits, and we were forced to reapply; we lived over a year with no governmental support. I was the breadwinner.

Despite working, running a household, and keeping us from homelessness or starvation, the best part of that awfully difficult year was that I managed to save up a thousand pounds to make that payment towards tuition fees the first year of university.

As neither my family nor my wider community wanted me to attend university, I was now challenging the status quo, and my own environment became quite violent. I was forced to do something that a young woman from the background that I am from would never do. I was forced to leave my father's house because of the violence towards me and my family's lack of support.

I had no choice but to leave home when I was violently attacked by one of my brothers, and he attempted to stab me in my shoulder. The build up to this moment was inevitable, I guess, as this brother had a substance abuse addiction (at the time). He had a loud voice when screaming at me on a regular basis to try to stop me from leaving home to attend university. At first, I was slapped around, pushed, and hit with items. I knew in my heart that one day something really bad would happen. When the stabbing incident took place, I made plans to take what I thought was important, such as clothes and food, and a few days later, I sneaked out of the house.

I went directly to university and stayed at the residence halls, where I was able to continue my education. It was during the first year after moving out that I fell into a lot of financial difficulty. I had become homeless, living rough on the streets of London after sofa surfing for a few months.

I loved my studying days, and I had an absolute blast. I met some incredible people and made some incredible friends. Those friends eventually became my chosen family. University allowed me to meet a range of people from different cultures and all walks of life. It taught me tolerance. University taught me how it's okay for people to have different opinions. It's okay for others to think what they want to think. It's okay if nobody agrees with what I'm saying. That was a complete contrast to the environment which I had just come from.

University gave me a place to finally be me. I finally got to decide, albeit nineteen years later, the kind of person I wanted to be and the type of person I did not want to become. I found that I was a very friendly person; I loved being around people and hearing their stories and views on things. University provided a very large crowd all the time, and I was friends with everybody. I had become friends with all people, from the janitor and the cleaner all the way up to the dean of the school. I was everybody's friend.

My mental health suffered tremendously due to all the trauma, and I cannot help but wonder what it does to one's psyche when someone goes through years of pain and hurt like I had. Here I was, spending all my life up to that point in an environment where I could never challenge a voice, an opinion, or even an idea. What I was hearing sounded odd to me. I was never afforded the opportunity to voice my opinion, to say what I really felt. When I did, it was like a slap on my face—I would be told I'm a troublemaker, a problematic person.

Then, at university, I was thrown into this new environment where in this world my voice mattered. My opinion now carried value. I learnt how there were so many different people in this world. With different customs, traditions, and cultures, and that they have different views and ideologies that were different from my own.

I was now in an environment where I was free to talk about that difference. I had the freedom to express myself, to understand I had the freedom to doubt or say what I wanted, to say something without fearing any repercussions. I had the freedom to actually voice my thoughts. I had the freedom to challenge somebody's opinion if I did not like it, or if I did not understand it, without being slapped in the face.

I learnt the art of agreeing to disagree. I learnt tolerance in multiple ways. Just because we may not always agree on something doesn't mean that we need to hate the person with that opinion as a result. I now had the freedom and luxury to listen to other people's opinions, to hear people's stories—how they have come through life and what challenges they faced.

University allowed me to grow and develop in ways that are hard to put into words as it gave me more than academia, a network of people, or technical abilities in the subject areas that I studied. It gave me so much more than just having those normal things. I only say normal because for everybody else, university is normal.

I gained so much more than all those things. I was finally in a place where I could breathe. I could just take a breath for as long as I needed to. I could go away and think about things that I'd heard, reflect upon them, and come back to ask follow-up questions.

I started to learn how other people had different customs, cultures, and traditions that would therefore influence their views on life and their opinions. It was incredible.

The most important thing, the real learning I really took away from it all, was the art of tolerance, the art of being respectful. Tolerance and respect are two things that everybody deserves as a basic right.

MARRIAGE

The main theme of my life was about escapism: escape from various types of abuse, escape from the constant negativity of being told that I was a waste of space and a regret. I would escape by imagining my life through my own fantasy world where I was actually accepted, loved, and valued as a human. Or I would imagine a world where I was neither told nor made to feel I was a mistake. I guess I was always planning and looking for an exit from all the drama that was happening around me.

That theme of escapism continued when I decided to get married. I had a very small Nikkah (Islamic marriage) in my mom's house with about twenty people. It was a difficult year because I had broken a few key friendships, so those friends were not with me at this time. I had lost some of my support system, and that made me even more desperate to get away from my environment and find an alternative. My mum was very uneasy about the situation and warned me to be careful before I took the plunge, but I ignored her. Mother's intuition is quite powerful. I was so adamant to have my way, to remove myself from the toxic environment I was in, that I responded to my mother saying that I was going to get married to him with or without her and the family's blessings.

I was always thinking of an acceptable way to exit my father's home, a way that would not bring cultural shame or give anyone in the community the opportunity to say that my parents did not raise an honourable daughter (again). The very concepts of shame and honour were ingrained in me from a young age, despite the fact that I did not know the real meaning.

When I was young, the way this word was taught to me was that anything outside of what was socially and culturally acceptable brought shame to the family. As I grew older, I understood that the way everyone described shame was just a way to control me. It was a way to have power over me. It was a way to ensure I followed their way of thinking and did not think for myself. This kept my mind busy and consumed a lot of me because I was always thinking, "How do I find myself an exit from this?"

As I matured, I could so clearly see how I had firmly anchored all my hopes of removing myself from an environment of constant negativity in marriage. Education would get me out of the house for only so long, but that would not work forever. It was quite clear to me that marriage was an escape route for me. It was an acceptable exit out of the situation that I was in, and I was so desperate to build my own family, to build a unit where I was in control, a life where I would finally have a say. Reflecting back now, I believe that desire played a strong role in me wanting to get married sooner rather than later. I wanted something that was my own, and I wanted to be part of a unit where I was welcomed, a place where I could be just me. I would finally be part of a family.

I wanted to be accepted as Nurjahan Khatun, who did not have to be everything everyone else wanted.

I was very close to my Baba, as I spent as much time with him as possible. He was also the only member of my family who was good to me; he worked very long hours, so he was out of the house for most of the day and never witnessed most of the negativity I had to experience. As he was unaware of this, I could not blame Baba for not doing something about the situation.

In my culture, the mother usually does most of the upbringing. Mothers teach the children discipline and ethics, and the men play a lesser role in the actual raising and teaching of manners. Fathers usually support disciplining the children, so in that context, Baba would not fully be aware of what was happening in the house. When Baba came home from work each night, I sought refuge in him, and he was absolutely my primary source of strength.

Baba passed away when I was only sixteen, and ever since then, I have always been looking for something to fill that void. The only time when I felt safe, secure, and happy was when I was around my Baba. I have always wanted to create something that gave me that same sense. Still do, to be honest. I wanted to build my own bubble where I had a sense of security like I had around my Baba. I wanted to build a family that was drama free. I felt that if I found somebody who had certain characteristics and traits that Baba possessed, then I would be okay. For example, I was looking for somebody who was family-oriented and knew how to treat women. Maybe then I could have my fantasy unit I'd been longing for.

Everybody was surprised when I came home and said I wanted to marry my now ex-husband. We were very different in terms of our personalities; my family was shocked as they had assumed, I would opt for someone who was well-established and settled in life. Because we were very different, we barely had anything in common, and it came across as though I was making a lot of compromises. In truth, I lost count of the number of compromises I made.

Traditionally, it is the girl who has to bear the brunt of the wedding costs. Instead, I wanted to use my hard-earned money towards a deposit for a house, which is exactly what I did. I had always wanted a small affair so I would not waste money on feeding hundreds of people. The marriage ceremony took place in my parents' house; the Imam (Muslim cleric) came over, delivered a sermon about marriage, and married us. My now ex-husband was all suited and booted and sat in the front room, and he came with a few friends to represent his side. The men were in the front room along with my mother, my uncles, and family members.

I was torn between doing what I had grown up seeing—arranged marriages where you learn to fall in love post-marriage, make all the sacrifices, and mold yourself into what the husband wants—and believing that I chose a good man who valued me and loved me for who I was. I wanted someone who would support me, uplift me, and empower me to love my life in a safe way and become a version of me that I was finally happy with. Wow. As I write this, I find it astonishing how I accepted so many wrongs from the very beginning of my marriage. I struggled to differentiate between what was culturally imposed on women and what a real partnership looks and feels like. That should have triggered the alarm bells for me, but I ignored them.

My now ex-husband never really had a career and always struggled financially. As a result, we discussed having children later as we were both so young when we married. We agreed to take our time to build up our respective careers and then think of kids once we were more settled. Additionally, he had responsibilities to his wider family, and he never had the academia to support his own career growth, which then ultimately put pressure on our marriage from the onset because he never earned more than me. I married in my early twenties, still relatively young and clueless, therefore under the illusion that "love makes the world go round."

Little did I know that it takes a lot more than love to make things work, as you need a regular income stream to be able to afford to eat, roof yourself, and clothe yourself. I had a very limited understanding of the world at the beginning of my marriage, which meant I was more than happy to fund everything and support my ex-husband. I had to accept that I was the primary breadwinner and did not consider the other support that should have come from him while I was the primary financial provider.

Up until I met my met my ex-husband, I was so used to being mistreated that I considered anything remotely nice he did as major. I believed him to be a good and kind person. He did look after me initially; however, looking back now, I believe he identified very early on that he could benefit from a marriage that was not really equal in any way. He was happy, content, and quite comfortable (and shameless, in my opinion) because he knew I would carry the bulk of the marriage. In the end, I was the one who carried the marriage financially and always had to manage the household activities.

Before my marriage to him, I had to buy not only my own engagement and wedding rings but his as well. It is customary for the bride's side to gift the husband with a wedding ring, but that felt unfair when I had to fund both sides. He told me at the time that he had encountered some financial difficulty and could not afford it. As we were both going against our families, we didn't want to admit to either of our families that we were financially struggling. In hindsight, I believe that was felt more strongly from my side, as I did not want to admit that we could not manage our own affairs.

I wanted to ensure that I came across as independent and avoided giving my family any opportunity to have a dig at me. I later learnt that my ex-husband's lack of money was going to become a regular theme. That alone should have said it all, to be honest. In my culture, asking someone else to pay is an incredibly shameless act. I covered that as much as I could and did not let anyone know that I was purchasing my own wedding band.

My marriage ceremony was quite a lonely affair because I'd had a huge fight with two of my best friends at the time, so they were not present during an important time of my life. That was particularly hard since we grew up together planning what we would do at each other's weddings. After some time, my best friends and I did reconcile and support each other moving forward. I had only one friend at my marriage ceremony; she came with her husband as they played a key role in being the mediators in getting my family to accept my ex-husband.

I had approximately twenty people at my ceremony, including a few family friends, immediate family, and extended family members. My Baba's best friend—Uncle Noor—and another cousin were the two official witnesses for the ceremony. As it was gender-segregated, the women were in the kitchen and dining area whilst the ceremony was taking place. When I was sat down on the chair to say, "I do," I distinctly remember looking into space and thinking, "Am I doing the right thing?" Everybody thought I was crying behind my veil.

I was not crying at all. You wouldn't find me crying. I wasn't going to be one of those brides who bawls her eyes out because she is leaving her father's home. I couldn't bloody wait to get out of that house. But during those ten or fifteen minutes, I remained silent. I didn't want to say, "I do." I knew in my heart that I didn't actually want to go through with it. In that moment I also felt the pressure of not being able to say no because I had created such a drama to marry this guy. I kept thinking, "Right, I have to go through with this now. How embarrassing would it be if I stepped away now?" In that moment, I managed to convince myself that it all was down to pre-wedding jitters.

I knew that coming back and living with the family again would mean I would be subjected to more abuse and taunting, and my life would be made hell. I had returned home for the greater good, and even though my inner thoughts from that moment were, "I don't think it's a good idea to go through with this," my heart was with my two younger sisters, whom I had missed so much. I wish I was strong enough to say, "No, I'm not going to go ahead with this," at the time. I consoled myself by saying that I was where I needed to be for the time being. Life at home was unbearable, and up to that point, life was very difficult for me—full of abuse and constant fighting. This was a good compromise and an acceptable way out.

In my culture, we are taught that if someone leaves home in an unfavourable way, it would impact the younger daughters in the family, and in my case, it was my two younger sisters. By this time, I had already left home pre-marriage. The community felt that I brought a lot of shame to the family, ruined my good name, and ruined my reputation, so I was viewed as a woman with no moral standing. When I left

home, the community constantly gossiped about how I left
home for one of three reasons:

- for a man/boyfriend,
- so I could go party all night and drink, or
- to sleep around.

When I came back, I had to agree to a series of rules,
promising that I would not do anything that would embar-
rass the family again. I had to give up any social life, and I
had to give up friends, so I started to lead a double life. In
front of the family, I had to demonstrate that I was abiding
by all one hundred and one rules. But I could not stop seeing
my friends—I mean, these are the very people who were there
for me, even more than my own blood family. There was
no way I would give that up. Getting married was the most
acceptable way to get out of the hellhole I was suffocating in.
I felt like this was the best way to go about it from a societal
point of view.

I thought, "How hard could it be to meet someone, fall
in love, and get married?" This would be easy enough to
remove the nonsense and drama I have always gone through.
If it wasn't for this need to leave and limit the impact on my
younger sisters, then I don't think I would have ever gotten
married. Up until that point, I was very anti-marriage based
on the fact that everything that I grew up witnessing in the
lives of married women seemed nothing but negative. Why
would I want to put myself in that position voluntarily? I
went from being very anti-marriage to saying, "Well, I'm
going to marry this guy just to get out," almost overnight. It
made sense to me at the time.

Due to all the broken and failed relationships I had with
family and friends, no one asked me, "Are you sure you're

making the right decision?" Looking back, I now know that mum had good intentions, but because I didn't trust her when I was younger, I didn't listen. Whatever she did say to me then came from a good place. Due to our volatile relationship, I thought it was coming from a place where she did not want me to be happy.

Having the right family structure and support who have your best interests at heart is vital, and when that is absent, you often make the wrong decisions. What drew me to this now ex-husband was the notion that I built up in my head that I needed a family-oriented man who was going to look after me and give me everything that I hadn't had up until that point.

When we met, he initially said all the right things when I was in pain or hurt by my family. He related, he showed me that he understood my pain, and he showered me with love. For example, if I had a craving, he would trek miles on a bus to get my favourite snacks, or he would make sure we had a date night every other week so we could just focus on us and distract ourselves from family drama. He was respectable, soft-spoken, and beloved by everyone. In turn, he developed good relationships with members of my family.

As I grew and matured into my own person, I slowly started to learn that you have to love yourself, make yourself happy, and be content with yourself first because no person can ever make you feel good about yourself or fill a void. No type of relationship can ever fill those voids for you. I gave that marriage everything I had, to the point where I was not nurturing myself anymore.

My ex-husband and I were like chalk and cheese. We were so incompatible, and in the first year of marriage, it started to become clear that maybe I had made a mistake. I felt I was madly in love; as my feelings for him grew, I became closer to him and attached to him. I guess I had slowly built my world to revolve around him and, soon enough, he had become my world as I felt more and more isolated from my own family, friends, and support networks. I truly believe he recognised that and took advantage of it as I anchored myself to him. My purpose of making myself happy and being in the driving seat of my own destiny—something that I had always wanted and fought my entire life for—had now vanished, and I was becoming one of those women I never wanted to be.

My sense of purpose became all about how to please him, how to keep my ex-husband happy. This became really unhealthy, and everything I did or said linked back to my ex-husband because my identity was attached to him. There were good moments, but soon enough, I felt like I did grow up. I confused what I felt for him and fell in love with an image I had built up in my mind. I considered that to be love, but I did not know any better. I cannot remember the exact moment I fell in love with him (or the image I had conjured up in my head), but I continued to watch his interactions with my family and admire the way he took charge of dealing with all the family matters.

Over the years, I saw parts of him change. He would not take my opinion into consideration, and he would keep shutting me down, becoming more controlling as I continued to grow as a person, developing a new hobby or interest. It was at these moments that I started to think, "Hang on, he wasn't like this before. Why is he behaving like this with me?" That created a tense undercurrent between us which exploded many years later. I know he loved me in his own way in the beginning, but as he saw there was a limit to how much he could mold and influence me, he changed his tactics and used me to benefit himself financially.

No matter what I did, it was never good enough. Sound familiar? Whether it was cooking, cleaning, ironing, folding, speaking, or making decisions, something could have been done better. It was impossible to communicate with him, as he had the world's worst temper and was always so angry. No matter what I said, he would always fly off the handle. I felt like I was constantly walking on eggshells. He had this strong passive-aggressive behaviour that left me feeling scared at all times. It got to a point where I would be too scared to even make a sound so as to not make him angry.

Back in 2012, I broke my left knee and was on crutches for over six months, and when he was working in the Middle East, I was lucky enough to perform the holy pilgrimage—or Hajj—to Mecca in the Kingdom of Saudi Arabia (KSA). All Muslims, unless they cannot afford to go, are required to perform a pilgrimage to the holy city of Mecca. This pilgrimage is one of the pillars of faith, and it includes a number of rituals and acts of worship that must be done in order for the pilgrimage to be considered complete. As a woman, I am not allowed to travel alone and must travel with a male guardian. A male guardian can be your husband, father, brothers, or nephews.

I initially travelled alone to Jeddah, KSA, as my ex-husband was already working in Riyadh. It was arranged that he come to Jeddah. Once I reached Jeddah, the first twenty-four hours saw him threaten me with divorce for the first time, and when I heard those words, I felt like I could not breathe. I suffered a crippling panic attack. Despite the time and effort I spent organising this holy trip, he was simply ungrateful.

He was cold and distant from me from the moment I saw him in Jeddah.

It was a difficult time in our marriage because things were so fragile. We were no longer connected in any way, so his trip to work abroad was not something I had anticipated, and it had come as a surprise. We had outgrown each other, had nothing in common, and more importantly, had no common goal. I realised much later just how critical it is in a relationship to have a common goal that both partners are working towards. I was reluctant to move to another country because London was home for me. When this pilgrimage trip came up, I hoped it would be a way for us to spend time together. I thought that we could potentially heal a few cracks in our relationship, and from the standpoint of faith, I wanted us to renew our intentions and give this marriage a real shot.

A few hours in, he started to pick a random fight with me, and that escalated to him saying he'd had enough and wanted out. To this day, I actually do not know where this pent-up anger towards me came from, as I had not experienced anything like this from him before. His words in this particular fight broke me. I had been trying so hard to make this marriage work, and now, without any good cause, he was saying he wanted to give up when he had never made any effort towards the marriage. I thought, "Why would he say such things to me in the holy land? He was the one who told me that we needed to give our relationship every effort."

The most hurtful incident I remember from that trip—which was indicative of how we lived our lives—was when we had to make the final visit to the holy mosque where you circulate the Ka'bah seven times; this is necessary in order for the pilgrimage to be considered complete. We were on the roof, and I was walking on my crutches as I chose not to hire a wheelchair. A few minutes into this act of worship in extreme heat, I felt my sugar levels dipping. I asked if he could get me some water to help me feel better, as I felt unable to continue. It was around this time when I was recently diagnosed with diabetes, and because I was diabetic, I could not have anything that had sugar, hence the request to grab me some water.

That was enough to make him angry. He cursed me and then left me in the middle of circulating the roof all alone. I felt like I was in a movie—a scene in slow motion—when that happened. I was dumbfounded as he walked further and further away from view, just like that. The crowd pushed and shoved me, starting to intensify. I needed his help to get me out of that crowd, as I was not able to walk. I had to use every ounce of energy and strength I had both physically and mentally to save myself so I didn't trip, fall, and get crushed or trampled, which was very common in these circumstances.

Each time I tried to move myself, I ended up getting hurt or being pushed back a few steps. I just was not quick enough because the crutches limited my mobility. That incident escalated very quickly, and I was trying to get down the stairs after what felt like forever. I had to find a way to get down a few flights of stairs, and I needed enough space to move at a snail's pace. All the while, I was praying so hard that I would not get pushed. I could not take a few steps down, and I felt the crowd pushing me from behind. Before I knew it, I had stumbled and fallen down the first flight of stairs. I was partially knocked out and bleeding.

The crowd pressure and intensity pushed me down a further flight of stairs. I was crying and screaming out in pain, asking people to stop pushing into me. I was being bounced around like a softball, asking those around me to help me in a language that they did not understand. If someone did want to help me, it would interrupt the flow of people moving down those stairs; therefore, it would be hard to help me without someone else getting hurt. I became more emotional as I thought of my ex-husband, who was not there to help me. In fact, this was happening to me because of him. One of the main reasons why male guardians accompany women to such pilgrimages is to care for and protect you from getting hurt. Meanwhile, my ex-husband was nowhere in sight. He had selfishly left me in my greatest time of need.

I stumbled down two flights of stairs and reached the bottom in quite a state. I had passed out, and when I eventually regained consciousness, some women and a few staff members were around me to help. The staff sat with me, wiped my tears, fed me a banana, and made me drink water. I just broke down, and one of the female staff members tried to console me. After a while, I managed to collect my thoughts and wondered, "Who the hell do I call? How can I reveal I am in this state when the first question others will ask me is, 'Where is your husband?'" I finally plucked up enough courage to call someone from the Hajj group I was part of to come and help me.

When I reflect on such painful memories, I now have the strength to admit I spent all my time, all my energy, all my intentions on making my ex-husband less angry during our marriage. Soon enough, I was molding myself into someone I could no longer recognise. I became nothing all over again. I became something that could no longer be described as a person. Nothing of Nurjahan Khatun was left by the time we were on this pilgrimage.

I look back and can see the way I did everything to please him only. I was convinced I had to make my marriage work no matter the cost. I had to prove to the world that I was successful in keeping my husband happy. The sad reality was that, despite my education, I had become everything I had fought so hard not to become when I was younger.

It was impossible to convey how he made me feel, and when I did pluck up the courage to share my feelings, he immediately interpreted my concerns as me complaining or being too aggressive. Suddenly, I had an "attitude problem." Soon enough, our marriage took me to a dark place—the place that I was trying to escape from all throughout my childhood.

I find out by accident that he had decided to apply for a job abroad without consulting me. I saw an email open on his laptop and some paperwork left on the desk. When I read it, I realised he had been applying for jobs, but I was not aware that he had been successful in one of these applications. He did not share what his intentions were. He must have realised I saw some of the paperwork that night, so the following morning, he brought up the topic.

It was a Saturday morning, and he casually mentioned how he has been successful in getting a great opportunity in KSA. I was stunned and shocked. I was unable to react or respond as I was trying to process what he had just said. He spoke about all the perks and benefits—that, for once, he would be earning more than me. He highlighted this point as it would be helpful to us if he could finally take over all the financial responsibilities. Additionally, he wanted us to try for a baby, and he suggested that once we got to KSA, we would try IVF treatment. That softened my heart a little.

All throughout my childhood, I was told I wasn't good enough. I was always told when I should speak, when I shouldn't speak, when I should eat, when I shouldn't eat, when I should sleep, when I shouldn't sleep, who I should engage with, and who I need to stay away from. Now I had an adult version of that attitude in my marriage. I could not have opinions. I could not have my own voice. I could not be myself. God forbid I shared my feelings and emotions or try to be assertive, as that was immediately misinterpreted as aggression.

As a brown woman in the workplace, you get told you are an angry person if you are assertive. You get labelled as aggressive, and then you come home, and you're told again that you're being aggressive. When I try to assert myself and create the boundaries that will help develop healthy relationships, I am told that I am being difficult or have too much of an opinion. Slowly but surely, that eroded away my personality—my soul, my character, who I was—and I found myself in the same situation as I was in growing up. I could not find my own voice. I could not be my own person. I could not live the life I wanted, one where I was free to make decisions, free to think and feel whatever I wanted to think and feel. I wanted a life where I did things on my terms and did not have to think of a hundred people at the same time. I found myself in the same cycle all over again.

I spent years of that marriage thinking, "What the hell did I do wrong? What did I do to make him like this?" When you are in an abusive relationship, you do not actually see the signs. He would treat me badly and then ask for forgiveness, and then I would forgive him. Then it would happen all over again. Before you knew it, years have gone by, and you have kept forgiving them just to get through the marriage.

He came across as charismatic and well-mannered, but he was narcissistic. It's something you just do not see immediately in a relationship, so I never imagined it to be that way throughout the marriage. I was so busy focusing on how to make him happy, how to make the marriage work, how to compromise myself even further in the marriage, and which part of me should die off slowly that I was blind to the signs.

I was blind to his controlling nature, constant taunts, and financial abuse—amongst other forms of abuse. I just did not understand how I had ended up in that position. I convinced myself for many years that I deserved it. Maybe because I was such a bad child or a bad teenager, because I was not a compliant daughter and sister, I deserved this. I spent so many years hating myself—far too many years telling myself that I deserved this, that I made him do this to me. I went back to a place where I told myself that I never deserved to be happy. I convinced myself that I was nothing. Therefore, I didn't deserve anything.

I tried my best to comply to his every whim with how I dressed, how I ate, who I interacted with, how I walked down the street, how I behaved around his family, and how I behaved around my own family. I became a "Yes, Sir. No, Sir. Three bags full, Sir" kind of person. I did that for so long. It was like he had a split personality: during the good times, he came across as supportive, encouraging, and supposedly always proud of my achievements. Other times, he went back to his controlling self.

A way for me to deal with the difficulties was to just throw myself into work and continue doing what I always do. I had to carry the relationship, whether it was financially or emotionally, which became a constant throughout the entire length of the marriage. I felt I was always making all the sacrifices—big sacrifices in terms of how I felt I was being loved as a woman, how I always felt restricted. I supported all his schemes and his desires, and with every ounce of energy in me, I always built him up.

He was one of those people who continually had new business ideas, and he would ask me for several thousands pounds, promising it would be the last time with each ask. But he failed at every single one of them, and it was me bailing him out each time, financially carrying him to my detriment. To be honest, most of the time I felt I had no other choice but to support him, and that was mostly due to fear— fear that it would cause a major fight and ruin the few days of peace I could have. I could not lie and say I didn't have the money as he knew what money I had.

I spent my money on maintaining the house, and in my culture, that is strictly a man's job. I did everything from A to Z. Meanwhile, every little thing that he earned was never re-invested in us as a couple. He ran up debts from before I married him, which he did not disclose to me. He had loans as he took money out. He would always tell me it was to support this family, but I could never really know if that was the truth. I had to always bail him out or top up whatever he was working on. He would send his money to his family, he had debt from before that he needed to pay back, and he said he was supporting his siblings—all that meant there was never any money for us.

We didn't want kids initially because we were both building ourselves, but I did become pregnant. I was pleased as I felt that a baby would help "fix" our marriage.

I had a miscarriage, and that crushed me. That crushed me in more ways than one. No words can ever describe that feeling—it crushed my soul forever. My ex-husband never really spoke to me about how he felt post-miscarriage; by the time I found out I was pregnant, I was quite far into my first trimester, and then the miscarriage happened.

I had no one to talk to about how I felt. My heart never mended after that miscarriage. It was already a difficult phase, but my troubles were further compounded by the fact I was also going through a breast cancer scare at the time. I never had peace at home, had nowhere to go, and had no one to speak to about my problems. After all these years, that miscarriage still weighs heavy on my heart and my mind. I still spend hours at a time crying and wondering what my baby would have been like if they had survived. A trauma like a miscarriage never leaves you no matter how many years pass by.

He was great at playing mind games, so we had plenty of normal and civil conversations, and other times, he would convince me the problem always lay with me—that he was perfect and never did wrong. He told me that the job opportunity in KSA would allow him to fulfil his role as a husband and that if I did not support him in this, then I would be the one preventing him from performing his role as a husband. He started to convince me that we could now solve all of the problems in our marriage because he associated all our marital problems with finance. He thought it was going to be easy: he earns more money, and our marriage is fixed. I mean, how could I reject that? How could I say, "No, I won't go with you," when I would be seen as the problem?

I initially did say no, and that caused a lot of fights between us. I felt I had no choice but to go along with it all because if I didn't, then that would mean I gave up on the marriage. Everyone would blame me for giving up and say I was being difficult. Eventually, I agreed with moving abroad as a final attempt at our marriage, and I agreed to try for a baby through IVF treatment. My ex-husband had always wanted a baby, and he had always wanted to become a father.

We did have civil conversations; he wasn't always fighting with me. But honestly reflecting back, we did not have healthy conversations. We were civil because I tiptoed around him and because I made all the adjustments and compromises. I was always the one who bent my back to make things work. I made all the sacrifices, and I was the one who lost myself throughout the duration of our marriage.

Going abroad was his dream. He knew being in an environment that supported and benefited men more than women was the only way he could assert full control. So, before I could go to the first IVF consultation, I found out that he had been cheating on me for some time. The multiple levels of betrayal I experienced made me suicidal. It crushed me. No matter how badly we didn't get on, I still felt strongly for him. I devoted my entire life to him. I sacrificed everything, pouring blood, sweat, and tears into that marriage to make it work, but I was pushing water uphill.

I couldn't stomach the infidelity, the betrayal, and that's what ultimately forced me to take a long hard look at myself and ask some really difficult questions.

"When did I let go of my self-respect?"
"When did I stop loving myself?"
"When did I start to believe that I could not exist without a man in my life?"
"When did I stop believing that I could not be independent?"

By asking myself these questions, I realised that I wanted my life back.

I wanted to be Nurjahan Khatun again.

I wanted to be able to breathe again.

I finally found the courage to make the decision that I deserve more.

I deserve a life with no abuse.

I deserve a life where I am not constantly walking on eggshells.

I deserve to be happy, safe, and content.

The infidelity broke our marriage. The trust, betrayal, and forgiveness are part of any marriage, and I had forgiven him for many things in the past up to that point. However, the way my trust was broken and how I was betrayed was the ultimate form of disrespect. Once that respect disappears, there's no way you can rebuild that. There's just no way. There's no way you could ever have trust again. There was no way I could forgive him.

Before, I was insecure, scared of him divorcing me, but the betrayal I experienced not only disgusted me but it also broke me into a thousand pieces.

I finally felt used and abused after all these years.

I finally felt that after ten years of putting up with everything, I could not put up with it any longer.

How could I be confident that he would ever have enough respect for me to not cheat on me again?

That was when I decided enough was enough.

I would not keep pushing this water uphill.

That's what ended the marriage.

I finally had the courage to dig really deep and ask myself the most difficult set of questions, like, "What have I gained in all these years of my life by serving others?" and "What do I need to do to make myself happy?"

DIVORCE

———

I finally agreed to uproot myself from everything and everyone I knew, try to set up a life in a new country, and stop flying between KSA and London.

My move was necessary in order to salvage the marriage, and I always wondered why my ex-husband chose to live offsite and not within the staff compound, especially as he chose to rent a five-bedroom villa with three lounge areas. I never quite understood why he decided to rent such a big villa, because our families were not going to be coming to visit us very often. I knew from the onset that my trip this time around did not feel right. I knew in my heart that it was going to be memorable. One particular night in that first week of my stay began the series of events that would unfold and change my life forever.

I noticed that my ex-husband was paying more attention to me than usual, and that left me wondering why I was being looked after, cared for, and loved up more than usual. I just assumed it was his way of starting to make things better between us, and I thought, *Finally, he is making some effort.* He went out of his way to take me out to dinner each night, wanted to take me shopping, bought me flowers a few times during a ten-day period, and he did not get angry with me like he always did. Little did I know that it was not for my benefit but only to ease the blow that I was about to receive. He ordered some takeaway, and we used the expensive china set he had bought with great pride. He wanted me to "just relax," so we had dinner and later moved to the sofa area as we were watching a movie on TV.

We sat on a tailor-made; expensive pastel sofa set that he was proud of getting. I had mixed feelings sitting on the sofa as it had been a few months since we shared a sofa space together, and my experience with him taught me a moment of peace like that can very easily be interrupted by his sudden outbursts of anger. He was displaying this new side of him that I had not seen before but only came alive when he moved to KSA. For him, it was all about show and tell. He had a point to prove to everyone how he had made it in life and how he had money, so he felt a need to demonstrate his success via his purchasing of materialistic goods and items. The main room was one of three reception rooms, and the main topic he would converse with me about was this villa—what he had bought for it and how he enjoyed its interior design. This room shared space with the kitchen and dining area and was meant to be the main entertaining space.

The air conditioning was making background noise as we started to watch a Bollywood movie of his choice. As I was about to settle into the mood and relax for the first time in a very long time and spend time doing something normal with no arguments, my ex-husband suddenly turned around and looked at me in this really intense way. I had not experienced this expression from him before; his eyes were looking deep, worried, and hesitant, and then I saw his eyes slowly filling up with tears. I had never seen my ex-husband cry before during the ten years we had been married. He held my hand tightly, kissed me on my forehead for a prolonged length of time, and then told me how much he loved me—that he was proud of me for being willing to make this marriage work, how he admired my sacrifice of quitting my job and moving to KSA to give my all to this marriage.

I thought maybe he would start to talk about how we need to make this attempt to save our marriage work and both of us should give it 110 percent. I thought he was going to tell me how we have been through so much together for the last ten years, and now was the time to dig deep and do what we had to do to make this work. My hands started to shake at this point while he was still holding them. His behaviour over the past week suggested that he was making more effort between us, and we had an IVF consultation booked, so here I was, thinking that he was really wanting to make this work.

For the first time, we actually spoke about the miscarriage I had suffered a few years prior; he spoke about how it had affected him, how it made him feel. He even asked how I coped, acknowledging that it had not been easy for me and my body. I had suffered very much health-wise prior to the miscarriage, and that event then took a toll on my body. Even two years after, it was still quite an ordeal for me.

A woman's intuition is a powerful ability; your gut feeling never lies to you. Despite having what I thought was a heart-to-heart, this overriding feeling was telling me that something bad was about to happen—a night where everything between us would change forever. I had this feeling in my gut that made me think there was a reason why he had been sucking up to me all these days. Sometimes your heart kind of knows when bad news is about to come, and when he sat me down, saying he wished to talk to me about something important, my heart told me, "Uh oh." Maybe what was about to leave his lips was not going to be good for me, for us, or for our marriage. I knew what was about to come out of his mouth would take us to a point of no return.

Something was about to come and smack me across the face and take the wind out of me.

He did not tell me anything about how we could make this marriage work. In one breath, he told me that he would do anything for me. In the next breath, he said he was under some difficulty that he needed my help with. He laid out a story about how his family was pressuring him to marry a second wife. He continued on about how his mother was going to choose a poor girl from a poor village who could give him, us, and his parents a baby. He wanted me to agree to a polygamous marriage. He wanted me to agree to him having a second wife whilst telling me how much he loved me, and I was his everything. We had been married for ten years, and he stressed that he needed to present a grandchild to his parents. His family wanted him to have a child to continue the family legacy, the family name, and the family's lineage.

As he said all this, I immediately started to clam up. I stopped breathing for a couple of seconds because I couldn't understand why he was saying this. I got this horrid feeling in the pit of my stomach, this heavy feeling on my chest as though someone had placed a rock on my heart. I tried to cough, but my chest only got tighter. I stood up to see if that would help, and I felt like I was having a heart attack, so my ex got me some water and a brown paper bag. I started to breathe into it, and after a while, I started to breathe okay again. He continued, saying he didn't want to go ahead with this but had no choice but to consider a second wife. He wanted me to give my permission. He kept saying he wanted my permission to go ahead with this so it would not tear the family apart. He said that if I truly loved him, then I would "take a hit for the family"—like we were some sports team, and I just needed to agree to take a knock to win a game.

I was perplexed at this point as the sole purpose of my trip over to KSA was to seek IVF treatment; it's what we agreed on prior to me coming over. IVF in KSA would be easier as we would be based there, but it would also be cheaper than in London. This was the case as back in the UK we had always struggled financially, and this was our opportunity to focus on having a family. With this new job in KSA, he was earning a lot more and on par with my salary.

I had provided so much to him over the years. He had used me for motivation, mentorship, and emotional support. He used and abused me in every sense of the word. He abused me financially and psychologically. He abused me in many ways as well as in terms of using me to always be his motivator. He drained my energy, so I called him the "energy vampire." Putting up with his controlling nature and constant abuse meant I slowly eroded away until there was nothing left of me. My personality was no longer there. Everything started to fall into place, and I realised that eroding my personality made him feel better about himself.

When I took a break from my career, I was taking the risk of having no income. I would have to ask him for money each time I wanted or needed something. As a result, I lived off credit cards and ran up financial debts because he was not providing for me.

By the end of that first night, when the whole second wife "discussion" came up, I just wanted to fall asleep and wake-up and hope it was a nightmare; however, by the time we woke up the next morning, I realised that it was not a bad dream. The news he had dropped on me was real, and the weirdest part of it was how he was behaving so normally. His behaviour went from one extreme to another, and the following morning, things kind of went back to the normal routine.

I got up, showered, and made him egg on toast and a cup of tea. I packed him some lunch, and then he went to work—just like that, as though nothing had happened. He came back from work, and I went up to him and said, "We need to sit and talk about what we discussed last night." His response freaked me out. His response to me made that pit in my stomach feel deeper, feel more real.

In the space of twenty-four hours, he went from, "I need your permission to marry," to him saying, "I don't think there's anything else that we need to talk about because it's something that my family is pushing for." What the hell happened to "I need your permission" and "I will only do what you agree with, baby?" That evening was awkward as hell as I tiptoed around him to avoid making him angry. He went back to his normal passive-aggressive behaviour, snapping at me, slamming things, and looking for any excuse to tear into me. I have no idea why I felt scared—maybe it was because I did not want him losing his temper on me.

I was carrying on as normal since I did not know what else to do. He was acting as though everything was fine which made me doubt if I was making this into a bigger issue than it needed to be, and lastly, I desperately wanted to believe that night never happened, so I was looking for some normality—however bad that norm was for me—and returning to the same routine. The saddest part of all of this was how the crazy, insane years of "dutiful wife" indoctrination from my childhood came in full force.

Then the following day came. I got up, showered, made him breakfast, and packed him some lunch again, and then he left off to work. He came home, and after I served his dinner, I said, "We still have not spoken about this, but we need to address it." This time, he snapped and bit my head off. I could not understand what was going on: two days ago, he wanted my permission, the previous night he said there is nothing to talk about, and then that evening he goes, "There's not really much more to talk about—Dad said I have to." When he said that to me, it felt like he punched me in the face. I was shocked. For two days in a row, his attitude was rapidly changing, and I could not keep up. I was left trembling at the response and the shift in attitude. My hands were shaking as I went to the bedroom. I just laid in bed, unable to react, to say anything.

The bedroom door leads directly into the lounge and dining areas, and I left the door open. I kept crying, thinking, *What the hell is going on?* An hour or so later, I could hear him on the phone talking to somebody for at least two-and-a-half hours. There's no one in the world you will speak to on the phone for two-and-a-half hours. *Unless it's a woman,* I thought. I couldn't fully understand everything that he said from a distance, but I clearly remember thinking, *He's speaking to a woman. He is trying to fool me.* I kept replaying in my head what had happened in the past seventy-two hours. I was unpacking in my mind the drastic change in him over the space of a few days. One moment I thought his tears were real and I had never seen him cry before. The next moment I thought how did he go from that to yelling at me saying there was no need for a discussion.

The rapid change in behaviour only led me to believe that he was already with somebody—maybe even already married to somebody—and there was an urgency for him to tell me all of this. Then I thought, *She must be pregnant, and he's due to have a child. That is something he cannot hide for long.* As he spent hours talking on the phone with someone I suspected was a woman, I approached him and said, "Who are you talking to?" He replied, "I'm talking to my sister."

I'm like, *There's no way you speak in a romantic tone with a sibling. That is not how you speak to a sibling, and what could you possibly be speaking about for over two-and-a-half hours with a sibling? It doesn't make sense.* I responded, "You are not speaking with your sister but to a woman." That night we went to bed in separate rooms after having another fight. I couldn't sleep all night as my gut told me something was not right. The following day, I got up, showered, made him breakfast, and packed him some lunch all over again, and then he left for work.

Over these few days, I had completely lost my appetite, living on only fruit and water. I could feel my sugar level going down but struggled to motivate myself to eat. On this particular day, something told my heart that I must search that villa from top to bottom to find any kind of evidence confirming that he already had another woman—something that would indicate that he was already married or having an affair. I was convinced that there would be something in the villa for me to find.

After a few hours of my search, I found clear evidence that he was seeing somebody, was married to her, and had even completed paperwork to bring her over to KSA! It had her picture and full personal details—absolutely everything. There it was in black and white. I had found the evidence that I needed to confirm that not only was he having an affair but also that he had gone ahead and married this woman and was planning to bring her over to where we were living at that time.

I took pictures of the evidence and put a lot of the evidence away in a safe place. I then waited for him to come home, as he usually did. The best way that I could get him to tell me what was going on was to force him to confess somehow. So, that afternoon, I texted him. I said, "Look, as you know, I have not eaten properly for a few days. Can we go to your favourite restaurant for dinner tonight? When you come back from work, pick me up so we can go for dinner straight away." That's what we did. I ordered my usual couple of dishes, and I encouraged him to speak to the owner, who was also his friend.

You have to remember this guy I married was all about show and tell and cared deeply about his personal image and how to project himself to others. I chose that place for dinner deliberately. I said to him, "I'm feeling really hungry. Can I order a few more items off the menu?"

He was pleased when I said that, so he said, "Yeah, of course. Whatever you want." When I finished eating my fill, I decided to order a couple of extra dishes because I had a little plan. For those who are not aware, everything is gender-segregated in KSA, so when you enter as a couple, you enter through what they call the "family entrance," where there are these portable walls to create cubicles in which families sit and eat. The waiter came and delivered all the extra dishes.

Being the direct, no-nonsense, cut-to-the-chase kind of girl that I am, I asked him directly. I said, "I know you said that you don't want to talk about this second wife topic, and you told me the past three nights that there is nothing more to discuss. I am not feeling happy with that response." I could see his face slowly turn red with anger as I broached the subject yet again. I then said to him, "I'm going to ask you a simple question directly, and I would really appreciate a direct answer. Have you already married?"

He denied it. I said, "I'm going to ask you once more. Have you already married somebody?" He still denied it, and I raised my voice each time. As he was denying it, I stood up and started to break each of those extra dishes onto the white marble floor. I threw each dish down onto the marble floor with more power, more passion, screaming at the top of my lungs.

It caused a lot of chaos and made the staff run towards our cubicle, asking if everything was okay. I kept screaming at the top of my lungs, saying to the staff, "Ask this man if he has married a second wife?"

You could see by the expression on his face that he was caught red-handed. I had now involved outside people in our problems, and he hated that because it embarrassed him. He ushered the staff away and snapped back at me, saying, "Yes! I have married somebody!"

"Why did you pretend and go for all this drama?" I asked. "Why could you not just tell me directly?"

When he responded, I was not satisfied, as my heart kept telling me that there was more to this story. You see, the way he kept changing his view on the topic three or four nights in a row made me ask another question. On the first night, he laid the foundation, giving me a sob story where he cried his heart out and said he needed my permission. On the second night, he said his dad was pushing for it. On the third night, he said this was no longer up for discussion. All of this just sounded off to me. Because of that sort of rapid movement, I was convinced that she was pregnant. I asked,

"Is she expecting?" And he denied it. I got up and smashed one of the glasses, this time creating yet another commotion. Again, a member of staff ran towards us due to the sound.

I raised my voice again and said, "If you don't tell me the truth, I'm going to start involving the owner of the restaurant in this discussion, so you better start telling me the truth."

He replied, "I'll tell you the truth—yes, she's expecting!"

I don't know what happened after that; the shock of it all made me fall to the ground, and I passed out. The next thing I remember was waking up in the hospital. The news of her being pregnant crushed me more than the fact he had married someone behind my back and had been having an affair.

I finally got home after staying at the hospital for a few hours for observation to make sure that I was okay. The final version of the truth was that my then-husband had already married somebody, and she was expecting his baby; it still felt surreal, like a nightmare. I mean, which self-help book can I pick up and read? How am I supposed to deal with this kind of news?

How do you balance yourself as an understanding wife and a woman who has done everything? How could you keep a marriage alive when you find out that your partner has not only cheated on you but also got another woman pregnant and married her? Now, I must stress as a Muslim that I accept the principle of polygamy if it is done correctly as outlined by our Prophet (peace be upon him).

How was I supposed to react when all I felt was pain, hurt, and betrayal, and I was unable to breath? I knew my marriage was falling apart, anyway. But what was all that elaborate drama—the over-the-top lies just to present himself as a saint and what he was doing for his parents as some good deed? What kind of person goes out of his way and plans such an elaborate lie to the extent that this drama unfolded over a few days? This was not the man I thought I had married ten years prior.

Once we came back home from the hospital, my immediate reaction was to go into the spare room and begin packing my bags. I told him to book me a one-way ticket back to London for the following day. As he stood by the doorway, baffled at my reaction, he spent a while trying to dig himself out of the situation. That, however, triggered our ugliest fight ever.

The fight was ugly because what transpired was a series of exchanges, primarily from him, that made me finally realise how during our decade-long marriage, where I believed that he was proud of me, proud of the causes that I supported and the work that I was doing, he in fact hated me. He could not stomach that I was more successful than him, that I earned more than him. Like a switch, the true colours came out that night. He was so bitter towards me inside. He absolutely hated me for my achievements and my successes. He hated that I did far better than him, both professionally and personally.

This was the ugliest fight, as I had discovered my entire marriage was one big lie. He was never really supportive of, loved, or even cared about the things I did or was involved with. He was screaming at me, and I was breaking things in the room, tearing up pictures of us together.

Everything that came out of his mouth was like verbal diarrhea. He listed problems: he felt I showed him up, outdid him deliberately, and strived to do better than him. Apparently, I used certain incidents to put him down. It broke my heart to have the person in whom I had invested so much time, energy, money, and emotional support throw all of this in my face.

It was a shock to my system because, all throughout the marriage, I had always picked him up. He did not appreciate or even acknowledge my ten years of carrying him, and it was because of my hard work that he made any progress. Wherever he was in life at that point was all off my back. It was due to my blood, sweat, and tears. It was because I funded everything. I've lost count of the number of his failed start-ups in which I invested in. Each time, he would beg me to invest my money into his stupid ideas so that he could try to make something of himself. I had always built him up on my back and to my detriment.

I sacrificed so much because I believed I was doing it for our future and to make him happy. Everyone around me thought I was successful, but what they did not know was that I was only applying myself at twenty-five percent. I underplayed my passion and abilities, so I did not outshine him or make him look incompetent. I stopped pursuing my own passion and my own desires, never pushing myself forward career-wise, just so that I could build him up. I believed that if I supported him, his success was my success.

He could not see me do better than him. He could not handle the fact that I was more educated than him. He could not handle the fact that he couldn't do any piece of work without my support. I only helped him because I wanted him to do better. I wanted him to have the motivation.

I thought by having my support it would help him learn to have self-motivation, but that night, judging by our exchange, I realised, in a very painful way, that he hated everything I stood for. Everything that I believed he had loved me for was actually the cause of his hatred. I'm not saying that we didn't love each other once upon a time, but over the years, that changed, and his love eventually turned into hatred towards me.

He hated the fact that I'm somebody who can build myself up by myself with no helping hand.

He hated the fact that when I had a bad day, I could dust myself off and just get back into the grind.

He hated the fact that I had perseverance and extreme levels of patience and tolerance.

He hated the fact that I was able to see things that he could not see.

I was a visionary. I have always been a visionary. I am one of those people that can go into an environment and see possibilities and opportunities. He hated me for that.

He hated that I had a list of contacts from a wide range of people with all different levels of influence, from all backgrounds, whether they were dignitaries or ambassadors who wanted to befriend me and spend time with me. He hated all of that.

He hated absolutely everything about me.

I was stumped, left thinking, *If this is how he has felt about me all this time, then which part of my marriage was actually true and genuine? Which part of my marriage was real enough that I could hold on to it and say, "I had at least X number of good years out of the ten?"*

He crushed me all over again. He said some of the most hurtful, degrading, and spiteful things to me ever. To hear them come out of his mouth shook me to the core.

I wholeheartedly believed that anything that he had was ours. Whatever I invested, sacrificed, and gave up was for the benefit of our future and for our family. It came to light that night that everything in which I had invested my time, energy, and money and the decade of sacrifice and compromise was all for nothing as he had other intentions. It was one-sided. He had basically used me as a cash cow.

He hated me.

He hated Nurjahan Khatun.

He hated the person that I had become.

From the moment he met me to who I was ten years down the line.

He hated the fact that I saw good in people.

He hated the fact that I would make seventy excuses before I would think badly of somebody.

He hated the fact that his wider family became very close to me and liked me.

He hated the fact that his family stayed in touch with me and built relationships with me.

He hated the fact that wherever I go, people just gravitate towards me like a magnet.

He hated the fact that I made use of every single opportunity that came my way.

He just seemed to hate everything about me.

What came about in the next few weeks was nothing short of pure pain. He had become quite obsessed with me accepting a polygamous marriage. The reason why he had rented a five-bedroom villa became quite apparent when I found the evidence that confirmed he indeed was having an affair and was married to another woman. He had paperwork planned and submitted to bring her over to our home in KSA.

That night, he refused to book me an air ticket. I did not have access to my phone because he had confiscated it. He had confiscated my British passport too. His controlling nature and his attempt to brainwash me into accepting a polygamous marriage led to weeks of mental abuse.

He kept claiming that he still loved me and that I was always going to be his first love. He said that he wanted to give the child that they were going to have to me, so I could raise it as mine. He wanted us to live a happily ever after scenario in this five-bedroom villa. He had all these plans and visions for the three of us to get along and live happily.

A few years prior, just after my miscarriage, I actually sat my ex-husband down and said that if he did want a second wife or to marry somebody that can give him a child, I would understand. By this point, several years into the marriage, I just knew how badly he wanted a child. When you love somebody, you're willing to do anything and everything for them. Women tend to sacrifice all, and I wanted to make him happy. I was willing to say, "Leave me and marry somebody else. Or if you want to have a child, we can find a way around it." If he had said yes, then it would have been done in an acceptable manner where everything was open and transparent—not by being sneaking, calculating, or being manipulative.

Fast forward to 2014—maybe due to that gesture I'd made a few years back, he probably thought that I would agree to all of that, but what he didn't understand was that when I offered such a thing to him at that time, we were both in a different emotional and psychological place. We were no longer in that space at this current time, as I would no longer consider that for a number of reasons. More importantly, the way he had betrayed me on multiple levels was evil and hurtful. He never had me at the core of his decision-making. Whereas when I had spoken of this a few years prior, I absolutely had him at the core of my decision, and I had considered all angles in my suggestion. It was not deceitful, and my actions came from good intentions.

Part of me would like to think that I've got a big enough heart to be willing to accept it if it meant we would have a family, but the way he went about it, how he betrayed me on every level humanly possible, was just unforgivable. The way he had planned something so sinister left me wondering if any part of this was sincere. I later found out that he had been planning this for over a year.

He spent the next four or five weeks deliberately trying to break me down mentally and emotionally. I cannot begin to explain what that felt like. I did not have access to anything. I could not ask or call for help. I just couldn't do anything. Eventually, I remembered that I had my work Blackberry with me by accident as I had left it in the internal storage compartment of the bag when I had taken a sabbatical from work and flew to KSA. I managed to use that phone to find out where I was, as I didn't even know my home address.

In the end, I found the courage to tell my ex-husband that if he didn't get my e-ticket in the next twenty-four hours, then he would be in trouble because I would have to be extricated from the country by the British government. His fear of getting into trouble with the authorities finally made him give in and book my ticket home.

I came home with the abaya (Islamic dress), a work phone, and a few belongings and stayed with a friend. I didn't go straight to my parents' house because I had done something that somebody in my position was taught to never do—leave their husband. I made up my mind on the plane coming home that I no longer wanted him in my life as my husband anymore. The next several weeks and months were horrific because I had no support from my family whilst trying to seek an Islamic divorce.

My immediate family was not supportive of me seeking a divorce, and until this day they have not even asked me what happened or why I did it. The community and extended family gave me a lot of grief as I was now labelled a divorcée, and that has much stigma attached to it.

Through this period of my life, I asked many of my friends to provide me with support, and the majority of them turned me away. They said that they did not want to get involved, and I learned how ungrateful people can be. I had always been there for others in their times of need, and the first time I was asking for help, they did not want to help me and did not even care. I asked them all once, twice, and thrice, but no one helped me. I had to find both the courage and strength to learn how to support myself and seek outside help.

Muslim women who decide to get a divorce are given this label of being a divorcée. Suffice to say, I experienced all the negative stigma associated with that term. I spent the first few years' post-divorce healing and recovering, rebuilding my life. Getting a divorce was the most difficult decision I had ever made. I fought so hard to marry him, and there I was, now divorcing him. Despite everything he put me through, I never thought I'd leave him. I thought I was going to spend the rest of my life with him.

I had to find myself all over again. I had to learn to stand up on two feet. I had to learn to navigate a world that did everything to put me down. I felt like that seven-year-old child all over again. I had nothing to my name. I lost every-thing, and I lost myself—my sanity—in the process. This dark phase of my life felt like it would never get better as depression and suicidal thoughts re-entered my mind and heart time and time again. It took me several years to come out of that dark place.

I had to work through my mental health concerns, seek professional help, get therapy, rebuild my support networks, and teach myself again that I was worth it—that I do not need a man to define me. I do not need a man to be able to form my own identity. It took me years of healing and recovering to get to this stage, but I did!

I felt so alone. I hated being alone. I spent my entire life being around people. Now, here I was for the first time in my life—in my mid-thirties and post-divorce—all alone with nothing.

I felt I had nothing to show for my life.
I had no financial freedom.
I had no emotional freedom.
Everybody was pushing me to go back to him.

I'm so grateful that something inside me never allowed me to let peer pressure bully me back into the marriage.
Somehow, I found the strength to be able to resist that and tell people, "No."
I knew what was best for me.
That was the start of my journey of healing and recovering for over three years.

The past few years, I have been feeling like myself again.
It is only in these past few years that I finally found my own identity.
Wow.

I made it.
I got through this difficult time.
I managed to pull myself out of this.
I hung onto hope.

CAREER AND SOCIAL IMPACT

———

I work in project delivery, which means I focus on making sure that programmes and projects are delivered in an efficient manner. Such environments suit my personality as the land of project delivery is incredibly varied; no two days are ever the same, and it allows me to work within a framework while staying creative and innovative. I am damn good at it, and I absolutely love what I do.

I never planned to enter the world of project delivery. I actually stumbled into it. Being the "fixer" wherever I go and dealing with crisis management for the family (here in the UK and abroad) ever since my Baba passed away put me in a really good position to not let things phase me. I do not get scared if a problem presents itself as my approach is to dissect the problem into parts and deal with it in a prioritised way. Pulling people in the same direction to deliver a common goal is something I have found myself doing really well, and I have learnt that I am able to influence others.

I had no choice but to look for a job at sixteen after my Baba passed away as we found out very quickly that no Baba meant no money. So, my very first job was working as a door-to-door salesperson for an American marketing company based in South London. I was one of those people who walked around in something smart-looking and carried this big black bag with different items in it. If I sold a little clock for five pounds, I would probably get about seventy-five pence commission.

I used to go door-to-door to businesses and retail shops, walking up and down high streets. By the end of the day, I might make ten or fifteen pounds, and on days when I exceeded my targets, I would make twenty pounds. That would be the money that I would bring home and use to buy food for the family, as we were struggling financially.

At the time, mum's government benefits were transitioning to something different, and her eligibility for benefits was under review, which took a long time to resolve. This sales job was a cash-in-hand job, which helped me buy food. I would work as many hours as I could in between college classes or on the days when I didn't have classes. I felt a big sense of responsibility to feed the family, as no one else was taking charge. The sole provider always ended up being me.

I realised I'm actually quite good at selling because I used to sell a hell of a lot. I realised just how competitive I am. Whilst in this job, I learnt some pretty good skills, like time management, being polite, and being tolerant. As this was an American company, a lot of emphasis was put on making your team members feel good. I learnt so much about the importance of teamwork and meeting joint targets whilst I worked for that company.

After a while of doing sales, I started temping in administrative jobs in the banking sector. I registered with many agencies, and I would get a lot of offers to temp around London. One of the offers I received was as a personal assistant

(PA) for a business centre for a local bank. Little did I know this would be the start of an important journey. The director I worked for picked up very quickly that I was excelling in my role, and he told me how he saw something in me. As he was a programme director with years of experience behind him, he told me I would enjoy stretching myself and getting involved in some project administration work.

That is how I stumbled into the world of project delivery, and I'm so grateful to him. He taught me a lot as he mentored me and provided me with opportunities to learn. His words of encouragement, saying that I can go really far in the future, helped me grow in my confidence. Those few years working with him really built my foundational understanding of what Project Life was all about. That's when I realised I actually was quite enjoying this career and wanted to continue in this space.

I felt more comfortable with my decision to pursue a career in project management the more I realised how organisation, time management, and planning were like second nature—thanks to my Baba for his militant style of planning. It came so naturally to me that I didn't have to waste time thinking about how to plan and organise; therefore, I then had time to focus on problem solving, fixing things, building relationships, and delivering.

I was able to juggle four jobs when I took my gap year. I worked a full-time banking job, cleaned toilets in the early hours of the morning and late in the evenings, worked as a hotel night receptionist on Thursdays and Fridays, and then spent all-day Saturday and Sunday doing fourteen-hour shifts in a local supermarket.

My undergraduate degree was in computer science, and once I graduated with my Master of Science, I worked in different industries. I took so much learning from each role

I had—the good and the bad. I was very successful in my private sector career, having worked in different project delivery roles across a range of industries. At the peak of my private sector career, my family circumstances drastically changed, forcing me to re-evaluate and consider applying for central government jobs to benefit from the flexibility and be more available around home.

My time in the private sector was very intense and very challenging, working within project delivery/IT/change environments. Being from a technical background meant I was working around very few women—even fewer than there are now. However, I did have great opportunities to work with many people, including teams from all parts of the world. I met many people whom I learnt so much from. I came across so many people I'd admire, and I was able to apply all that I had learned from my time in the private sector when I moved into the civil service. Working in civil service provided me a space to continue my love of learning while I struggled to adjust and adapt to the culture—the world of bureaucracy and red tape. I have gained the skills to overcome challenges that are laid out in front of me.

After five years of being a civil servant, I had a job lined up to go back out in the private sector because I had taken a demotion and felt like my career was going backwards. I found the civil service life was just becoming too difficult and thought I'd never settle in. I always felt quite frustrated because I ended up doing things I hadn't done for five years in my career. I was feeling unfulfilled. People around me knew nothing about project management, and I always ended up knowing so much more than them. In addition, because I did not have a supportive line manager, it became difficult to progress in my career.

Unfortunately, circumstances at home did not improve, and I was not able to move back into the private sector. That was the moment I made the decision to make civil service work for me. When I made the decision to make this work for me, I just naturally progressed through the ranks over five years until I reached the position that I'm in now.

It's been a challenging journey in the second half of my time in the civil service as I kept breaking through many perceived glass ceilings to get to the position that I am in now. One thing that I've learnt throughout my career is that many people will try to project their own insecurities onto you.

Many people will doubt your ability, question your competency, and make you sound like you're mad because you're innovative and you're creative. One thing that I always maintained was my authenticity. I always stood by the decisions that I made. I always knew that I was being fair and just in how I conducted myself and pursued certain things. I made sure that I allowed everybody to become part of that journey. I communicated well with people.

Wherever I went, I was able to inspire and motivate individuals regardless of age, background, or rank. I learned from my time in the civil service just how much I was able to give back and how much I enjoyed giving back. That's how I was able to take my professional career and learning expertise and transfer all of that into the work that I started to do outside of my day job.

How I grew up spending time with my Baba intrinsically influenced my own value system. Seeing and being involved in all the help my Baba gave others left such a mark on me and my life. It has made me want to do the same and help as many people as possible. I am sure there is some science that will explain why I ultimately want to follow in Baba's footsteps. I want to help people either directly through the various projects I am involved in or indirectly through other work I share.

My own value system around love, respect, and treating others equally has always been central and core to everything that I do. With every person I help, my value system is reaffirmed. I always try my best to give back to my communities. I believe I have been fortunate enough to receive an education, to have the experiences I have shared and many that I haven't shared, and these always drive me to look for ways to make an impact.

One of the more direct ways I found to give back that has enabled me to work with different communities is by supporting vulnerable people on an individual basis. This has been the bulk of the work that I've been doing since I got back on my feet after my homeless experience. I have supported women as they flee domestic abuse and served those who are experiencing homelessness at soup kitchens.

When I started this work over a decade ago, I never saw any of my own communities focusing efforts on those who need help locally. During the first few years that I did this work, there was hardly anybody who looked like me. I had the pleasure of working with amazing public organisations, churches, Christian missionaries, Hari Krishna centres, private organisations, and individuals to be able to have a far greater reach with regards to serving the homeless.

I then found opportunities to get involved as a volunteer TV presenter on two satellite TV channels where I had the opportunity to address a broad range of subjects that my communities did not necessarily want to talk about. Whether it was to discuss homelessness, domestic abuse, sexual abuse, or child sexual exploitation, I was grateful for the opportunity which that platform gave me to give back.

I was recognised for my efforts back in 2017 when I was given a very prestigious industry-recognised award for transferring and applying my professional skills to all the work I do to uplift women—in particular, my ability to help individuals become self-sustaining and self-reliant so that they do not depend on governmental benefits.

Over the years, I have become more and more involved in social impact work as people are so important to me. Knowing that I can in a small way contribute to others progression, success, or happiness genuinely fills me with joy as that means I am playing a critical role in spreading love and hope. I absolutely love being able to connect to people in such a way.

While I was homeless, I would plan how I would want to be able to support other women who may have gone through experiences similar to mine. That is when my idea for a social enterprise was born, and I have delivered, impacting over two hundred women as of 2021. The social impact focuses on working with women from disadvantaged backgrounds (economic, social, and cultural) regardless of race, religion, or ethnicity. Additionally, it helps women identify their aspirations and instils in them the belief that they can unlock their own potential.

I have both the belief and vision that the empowered women of our world can achieve and live their dreams. My work has dared women to do what they have been afraid of doing due to lack of confidence, inspiration, resources, or a combination of these limiting factors. Leadership training, mentoring, and coaching not only empowers women to seek to fulfil their aspirations but also inspires them to reinvest in their communities by mentoring and supporting others in similar situations.

I have always enjoyed working with women and encouraging them to unlock their potential and achieve their dreams through the art of storytelling in workshop settings.

The majority of women I have worked with come from communities that have either given up on them, judged them, or have not provided the support and encouragement they require to motivate themselves to doing something productive with their lives. Thus, these women may not push themselves, or worse, they give up completely. These women had not been inspired to give back to their own respective communities and make positive contributions to improve the places they come from.

The concept of this work is that those who have been through this journey come back and become a source of inspiration for new women entering the journey. This is how I demonstrated to other women that they too can dare to dream—I provided them a hook of hope, telling them that they can find that courage within themselves to do so.

This has created a powerful chain of positivity, benefitting the individual today and enriching society tomorrow. Women outnumber men in most countries, and they have consistently and repeatedly excelled wherever they have been given the skills and opportunities to contribute. When they are given hope, they will succeed in growing their communities, their families, and general development.

Society that requires articulate, empowered, and visionary women encourages capacity-building. Providing a private and safe space for women to network, believe in themselves, have hope, and share a platform with other like-minded women has caused women to make phenomenal strides.

What I have been able to achieve with women so far works, and my dream one day is to do this full-time as I have seen the hundreds of women my project has supported to date. I feel immensely proud of how so many women have gone onto setting up their own enterprises, have become self-sufficient, and are giving back to society. Women who have positively impacted their immediate family and their local communities. They have become a model citizen, and educating the younger generation to adopt qualities such as perseverance and dedication.

The work I delivered in this space was and is still crucial for bringing back humanity and supporting women as they become the movers and shakers. You might ask, "Why?" Well the social impact I do brings great benefits like:

- Women believing in themselves through improved and increased self-confidence.
- Improved employability prospects.
- Improved understanding of their own strengths and weaknesses.
- Positive contributions back to society.
- Active participation in the community.
- Women going on to higher or further education.
- Setting up enterprises.
- Raising awareness of the multiple issues that women face.

The way I give back now is through my work environment where I support, uplift, and empower others through mentoring and coaching. I try to share my journey as much as possible to show others how everyone has a role to play in setting the direction of where they wish to travel for their careers. Every single one of us should pay it forward by supporting others and uplifting those around them. Only through this will we ever truly empower each other.

Being a huge fan of storytelling, I have learnt from my own difficult lived experiences that I must be in control of my own narrative and want to tell my own story—not for someone else to share a version of my story that I do not necessarily agree with. I have learnt throughout my career how, in order for me to truly grow and develop in a competitive environment, I must seek my own opportunities so I can really stretch and be a great leader.

My love for storytelling is why I often talk about allyship and its importance. Irrespective of where you are and what environment you are in, it's on all of us to shed light on allyship. It is important to explain how someone with privilege and power seeks to first learn about the experiences of a marginalized group of people. That is how it ultimately empathizes with their own challenges and builds relationships with that group of people. I truly believe this is critical in overcoming the common challenges that many of us experience.

During my career, I looked for talent programmes and found opportunities where I could learn to be a better version of myself. I acquired knowledge and built my networks and contacts so I would always be in the position to share my own story.

The struggles I had to endure during my career journey—such as breaking through multiple glass ceilings and doing the hard on the ground work over the course of almost two decades—have taught me a lot about language and how others respond to me.

By understanding my own purpose and what I want to achieve, I stopped letting what others think of how I sound affect me in a negative way. It taught me how to hold myself accountable so I do not let anyone deter me from my purpose. That allowed me to grow, develop, and dig deep into evolving into the person I am. This was incredibly powerful, as I became more and more comfortable in my own identity.

I carved out my own space in all of this, and the more I grew, the more I embraced my so-called "flaws" as my uniqueness. I became confident. I was the version of myself that *I* had defined. I became totally and unapologetically myself.

HOPE

Healing and recovery were two words that I had never really paid much attention to, though these were two words that would become part of me and who I am now. They were two words that took me a long time to accept, digest, and then take action towards. They were two words that took all of my energy in those first three years post my Islamic divorce. That was a really dark time for me. I had no support; no one in my family truly cared what I was going through or took an interest in me. Those years were so lonely as I learnt the hard way that my family and my so-called friends were not who I thought they were. When I was barely functioning, no one wanted to know. I was too much work. They would finally have to make an effort, and I learnt I could not count on anyone but myself.

For the first time in my life, I was forced to ask for help as I recognised that I may not be able to pull through this all alone. Each time I reached out to ask for help and was let down, more of me broke. That constant cycle of asking for help, being let down, no one showing up for me, and having my heart broken was devastating; however, within that devastation, something quite beautiful blossomed. I grew, I became stronger, and I was not dependent on anyone but myself. I spent my entire life being dependent on others around me, and now, I was suddenly all alone. I had no family, no real friends, no husband, no nothing.

I had to sit myself down in those first few weeks of being alone and do what I do best: draw out a plan and plan my way out of this. Being a visual person, I drew on a piece of paper all the different elements that were flying around in my life so I could just capture it all and see it in its entirety. That was when I realised just how much I was holding in my mind; how much I was pushing myself to deal with everything at the same time with no prioritisation. Once I had captured it on paper, I was able to look at it all in a sensible way. I then approached it as I would any project.

This sounds weird, I know, but all I could think of doing was applying my skills and tackling this as I would do in a work situation. It gave me a sense of worth, to be honest. Planning gave me a sense of belonging, as I knew the steps I would have to take to address my struggles. I started to feel like I had a glimmer of hope, as everything was exaggerated in my mind. Once I got that out of my head, it meant the problems were not all as big as I felt they were. That level of familiarity is what started to slowly give me confidence. The process to heal and recover started when I wrote that plan, and then a few weeks later, I was sharply reminded that I had more time on this planet—that I had to go through this to come out better by the end of it.

After I left my ex-husband in KSA and returned to the UK in November 2014, I went away with a friend to begin processing the divorce journey on which I was about to embark. I took some time out and went away to North Africa in the hope that it would clear my head and allow me to get my thoughts together to brace myself for all the backlash I anticipated. I needed to pluck up the courage and notify my family of my decision to divorce my husband. On that first evening of holiday, my friend and I started planning the itinerary for the rest of our time there.

We left our hotel room that morning, taking all our holiday money and our passports in our purse. On the first full day, we made our way to the spa and spent the day pampering ourselves, including some type of body wrap, a massage, and making use of the jacuzzi, sauna, and steam room. As we would go to this particular resort often, we got to know the staff, met our holiday rep, and booked in all our excursions. Whilst we were getting pampered that morning, we entered that last stage of the package, getting a massage. I was on the massage bed furthest from the door, and my friend was closer to the door. As it was lunchtime, the two members of the staff said that they would go have their lunch whilst we relaxed and that they would return in fifteen to twenty minutes.

I fell into a heavy asleep whilst we were waiting. Suddenly my friend woke me, saying I needed to get up and get out. At this point, I was unable to make out what she was actually saying. I tried to lift my head up, but it felt like I had bricks weighing me down. I could hear my ears ringing and a faint voice. I could also feel my friend shaking my arms and body. I tried to lift my head up again and with great effort I lifted myself from the massage bed. The room was spinning, and my vision was not very clear. I could hear my friend screaming, "There's a fire! Get up! We have to get out!"

Everything was in slow motion at this point. I felt like my body couldn't move any faster. I wanted my body to move faster, but it just wouldn't. I managed to get off the massage bed, and as I put my feet on the ground, the room was quite smoky. As the ringing in my ears subsided, I could hear my friend saying, "Wrap yourself with a towel. We need to get out of here." I could not see her; I could only hear her. At this point, I could just smell smoke, and my head felt heavy and very groggy. The sound slowly became louder, and my ears popped. I looked to my left, and I saw this raging fire in the corner of the room. I could not believe my eyes. I was in shock.

I wrapped the towel around myself as I felt a sense of panic sweep across my heart and body. I kept thinking, *I need to get out of here.* By this point, I can only assume my friend managed to get out, as she was situated closer to the door. We had left our handbags, which had our passports and money, on these two hooks that were near the fire. I stupidly wanted to save those, so I began foolishly and instinctively making my way towards those hooks. I grabbed the bags and burnt my palm as the straps of the handbags went over my arm.

It was at that moment that I heard the first explosion. It wasn't a huge explosion, but it was enough to make my head feel like it was going to explode, and a fresh wave of fire and smoke smacked me across my face. I felt like I lost my orientation. I wasn't able to figure out where I was. Suddenly, I lost my bearings, tumbling over backwards. The fire was black and dark red, engulfing the ceiling and the corner where the steam room and sauna were. Then the second explosion went off, and this time, the steam room glass exploded, and I felt I was part of a *Die Hard* movie as the force of that explosion threw me towards the back of the room. I hit the wall and fell. I felt these shards of glass on me, on my face, and on my arm. As I hit the wall, I banged my head and fell to the floor.

I tried my best to move, but I couldn't. I tried to cough, as I was now struggling to breathe. My eyes were burning, and

I could feel the smoke was at the back of my throat, burning my throat. I was trying to scream for help. I don't know if I was making any sound or not, but I continued to scream. I remember thinking, *I need help.* The more I tried to keep my eyes open, the more it felt like something was shutting my eyes. I was running out of energy, and it was at this time I thought, *I'm going to burn to death like this. This is my last moment. What a way to go out.*

I started to pray that prayer you say before you die as a Muslim, and I kept on reciting that prayer as my eyes were closing. Then I saw this flashback that left me thinking, *If I die, how will my mum cope? If I die, what will my sisters do? They're so dependent on me.* All of a sudden, I found this burst of energy, and my eyes opened. At this point, because I was on the floor, I could see the legs of the massage table and what I believed to be the door. In the background of all this is happening, I heard commotion and screaming in Arabic. With that sudden burst of energy, I did a *Rambo.* I quickly tightened the towel around me, and then in true *Rambo*-style, I used my upper body strength to make my way towards the door. I dragged myself and my tired body to the door.

When I came out of that door, I turned around, and all I could see was this raging fire, spitting out black and red. It was all over the ceiling, and I thought, *How did I manage to escape that?* It was the scariest thing I have ever seen in my life. I tried to stand up, but I immediately fell down on the floor again because the wall I was touching was so hot. Then I saw a handle because there was another door to the left, but that was a dead end as that only led to the communal jacuzzi area. Luckily, I could hear screams, and I could hear my name being called. Lights flashed. A member of staff covered me, handed me some wet towels, and escorted me out.

***

It took every ounce of energy and sanity in my body to leave such a difficult marriage and to make the monumental decision to get a divorce. But I managed to leave an abusive marriage, and I was going to do what I believed was best for me. I kept thinking about how I had left a traumatic environment, managed to get back home to the UK from KSA, and then almost burnt to death. I had just survived a near-death experience, so I took that experience as a divine message telling me it's not my time yet.

That incident was a huge wake-up call, and it provided me with the clarity I was seeking. It helped give me that extra confidence I needed to go through with my decision. I got another chance in life. I got another opportunity to experience all the beautiful things that I had not yet experienced. I was never allowed to experience my childhood, and later, I never really got to experience life whilst being married.

What this incident did was teach me how I must have hope, and I must continue to hang on to that hope. It showed me that life can be beautiful, even after a traumatic experience. How you behave, how you conduct yourself, and how you carry yourself play a huge role in how you move forward.

Another example of when I was given a new lease on life was a few months after the fire incident. In 2015, I took my mother to Bangladesh. We were there for a month; I go as often as I can, as both my Baba and my eldest brother are buried there. We live in a remote village ninety minutes away from civilization, and the house that my Baba built is near my maternal grandparents' side. There is this little stream that separates the houses, so I would regularly pop over to see my grandparents. My only maternal uncle lives at my grandparents' house, which is made of tin and mud. Opposite that main house is another home that has now been built for my grandmother. They were doing some construction work during the time of this particular visit because my uncle was building a simple two bedroom few storeys. I would regularly go sit up on the roof to dry my hair away from people.

On this one occasion, I was on the roof and had taken off my headscarf, sat in the sun as my hair dried. The stairs in the middle of the property were still exposed, and kids were always playing in that area, which was very common in village life. Some kids had been playing with a form of liquid, and to me, it looked like water as they had filled water balloons with it. The stairs went across the whole floor and directly up the roof, which had a lot of materials and tools lying around. It looked like a construction site.

Whilst was I on my way to come down from the roof, I accidently stepped into some of this liquid, and my foot slipped. I slipped in such a way that I went flying off the building, and I fell splat onto the ground floor and onto some stairs.

By the way that I had fallen off the building and the way I had landed, I should have been dead. I hit my head, and my body was in this weird position, so everyone said that I should have been broken into several pieces. Everybody thought I was dead because there was no way I could have survived that fall. My legs were bent in different directions and my head was bleeding, so everyone freaked out.

When I finally regained consciousness, a doctor was examining me. The bleeding was coming from the cut on my head. Luckily, nothing was broken. I sprained a few things, was heavily bruised, and had these scratches everywhere. But I didn't have a single broken bone. Everybody called it a miracle, as there's no way I could have survived that fall.

I felt it was yet another divine message telling me I still have more to give back to this world and so much more impact to have on others. I can help others—give them the tools and techniques, the confidence and power. I can help those beautiful people who are feeling stuck in a rut and like they cannot get out.

I've got more time to say to people around me how I understand their pain.
I understand how they are feeling, and I'm here to help.
I've got so much more to give to the world.
I've got so much more to give.
Over a time period of three to four months, I had two near-death experiences that I should not have survived.

Hope allowed me to overcome those traumatic experiences mentally, emotionally, and physically.

Yes, every situation in which I found myself throughout my life has been challenging. Yes, they have made me think, "Why is it happening to me?" Yes, I could have given up, but I never did.

When I was younger, I attempted suicide on two separate occasions, and both of those times, I was unsuccessful at ending my life. I have resorted to self-harm for many years, hid my depression, hid my anxiety attacks, and hid my suicidal thoughts, but despite going through these, I still had this overwhelming feeling to have hope—to hold on to hope.

As I have grown and my understanding of life has evolved, I have had less of those suicidal thoughts. I learnt how life is precious, how life is a gift. In the second half of my life, as I matured into adulthood, I started to learn the tools and techniques to help me cope and be in control of my reactions and my responses. I had to spend years learning to accept that I have no control over what others do and say. I had to learn that I was wasting my time by getting upset over those things over which I had zero control over.

I learnt how life is about ups and downs, and that there will be highs and lows. I have had many dark moments as I struggled to learn to cope with life. One of those lows was when I suffered a miscarriage after spending many years trying to conceive a baby. I remember how culturally everyone was blaming me, the woman, who is seen by default as solely responsible for whether a couple can have a baby. Others made the automatic assumption that there was something wrong with me. I had to constantly endure insults from both in-laws and wider society, which was just unbearable and made me think that I was worthless—that I did not deserve to be happy. I thought having a baby would fix my marriage and make everyone around me happy. That period left me feeling like I was less of a woman and therefore didn't deserve to live anymore.

Another dark moment was when I decided to leave my ex-husband. The lack of compassion and empathy I received from my immediate family, extended family, friends, and the wider community was painful. Again, I was constantly made to feel that my life was nothing if it did not have a man in it. I battled a deep depression alone, and again suicidal thoughts overcame me. It took me over three years to heal and recover, but I have come back stronger than ever.

In all the examples I have shared, all I ever wanted was for someone to ask me how I was, if I needed any help, and rally around me to help me. People do not uplift one another or empower others enough. We need to help each other find the ability to hope and believe things will get better.

What I learnt more recently over the past few years is that having a soulful conversation and confidence about being different is so powerful as that could propel you into greatness. Confidence may not bring you success in general, but it will give you the power and the tools to face any challenge in life—*anything*. We will look back on life or periods in life, whether they are positive or negative, and have many regrets; however, I have always been able to look back on my tears and laugh.

What I'm trying to say is that the right things to do aren't always going to be the most popular choice according to the majority of people or to those you know. Be proud to be different, learn what it means to have authenticity, and be authentic. Get comfortable in being you but be real in being yourself. No matter how different you are, just be real in being different. So, if I'm in a room full of normal individuals, I can be myself, and I can hold my head high. I can be a rose in a field full of dandelions.

A few years ago, someone told me something. That person said to me, "Nurjahan, be ineffable." That word has stuck with me since, and wherever I go, I am ineffable.

ACKNOWLEDGEMENTS

———

I would like to thank all my Indiegogo supporters:

Lindsey Marks

Amal Makki

Usman Kasser

Sally Beeson

Arielle Hanien

Danny Richmond

Amal Gailani

Sadia Malik

Samantha Rockey

Mira Vyas

Amina Uddin

Halima Mohammed

Andrea Hodos

Sadia Ali

Jake Hayman

Anneessa Mahmood

Leticia Corbisier

Tim Banfield

Sadia Mirza

Azizur Rahman

Yuri Sasson

Margarida Saragoca

Lisa Gossels

Tim Fenemore

Rose Anderson

Dieuni Welihinda

Rrima Shakeir

Charlie Andrews

Belinda Wong

Naheyd-Akhtar Malik

Sophia Zisook

Deepak Rawal

Emre Kazim

Shehnaz Koria

Sunita Bali

Michelle Leong

Sonam khan

Ferha Syed

Jacquie Lewis

Samira El Messaoudi

Kevin Barrow
Manezza Malik
Sabina Khanom
Forhana Begum
Eric Koester
Kenza Aloui
Kerri Read
Dimple Patel
Meena Haque
N Khatun
Saema Rangrez
Atiya Aftab
Zahra Latif
Sonam Nawaz
Saddaf Kiani
Nazia Rasul
Julie Rahman
Saira S
Jackie Barnaby
Chantelle Johnson
Ansa Shabir
Mazena Doskal
Cassandra Flavius
Dilara Khanom
Shazama Manir
Linda Sadiq
Masuma Begum

Farhana S Karimabadi
Saudah Ibrahim
Bernadette Thompson
Rosie Grant
Hiren Dhimar
Sarbjit Sidhu
Silvester Aina
Sahir Bashir
Mehwish Malik
Saima Rasool
Mujahed Sebai
Anil Dutta
Shazia Nazir
Sadia Salam
Sana Chaudhry
Nosheen Malik
Linda Obiamiwe
Ruby Shakera
Alexander Goldberg
Goobi Kyazze
Isobel Platts-Dunn
Birahim Mbow
Manthitan Massita
Hardeep Atwal
Darren Patel
Alvena Kureshi

Printed in Great Britain
by Amazon